THE PSALTER

THE PSALTER
PSALMS AND CANTICLES FOR SINGING

CHOIR EDITION

Compiled by Hal H. Hopson

© 2011 Westminster John Knox Press

First edition
Published by Westminster John Knox Press
Louisville, Kentucky

11 12 13 14 15 16 17 18 19 20—10 9 8 7 6 5 4 3 2 1

All rights reserved. No part of this book may be reproduced or transmitted in any form or by any means, electronic or mechanical, including photocopying, recording, or by any information storage or retrieval system, without permission in writing from the publisher. For information, address Westminster John Knox Press, 100 Witherspoon Street, Louisville, Kentucky 40202-1396. Or contact us online at www.wjkbooks.com.

Scripture quotations from the New Revised Standard Version of the Bible are copyright © 1989 by the Division of Christian Education of the National Council of the Churches of Christ in the U.S.A. and are used by permission.

Every effort has been made to determine whether texts are under copyright. If through an oversight any copyrighted material has been used without permission, and the publisher is notified of this, acknowledgment will be made in future printings.

Book design by A-R Editions, Inc.

PRINTED IN THE UNITED STATES OF AMERICA

∞ The paper used in this publication meets the minimum requirements of the American National Standard for Information Sciences—Permanence of Paper for Printed Library Materials, ANSI Z39.48-1992

Westminster John Knox Press advocates the responsible use of our natural resources. The text paper of this book is made from 30% post-consumer waste.

ISBN: 978-0-664-23704-2

CONTENTS

The number in parentheses is the selection number in the full edition of The Psalter: Psalms and Canticles for Singing *(Louisville, KY: Westminster/John Knox Press, 1993).*

Preface 7

Psalms
1:1–4, 6	1	(1)
5:1–8	2	(4)
8	3	(5)
23	4	(20)
24 (Israeli Folk Melody)	5	(21)
24:1–6 (Hopson)	6	(22)
27:1–6	7	(25)
30:1–2, 4-5, 11–12	8	(27)
34:1–10	9	(32)
36:5–11	10	(34)
42	11	(37)
43	12	(38)
47	13	(42)
50:1–6	14	(45)
51:1–12	15	(47)
62:5–12	16	(52)
63:1–8	17	(53)
65:9–13	18	(56)
67 (Gregorian)	19	(59)
67 (Eastern Orthodox)	20	(60)
70	21	(62)
72	22	(65)
78:1–4, 12–15, 23–25, 29, 37–38	23	(67)
79:1–9	24	(69)
80:1–7	25	(70)
82	26	(73)
84:1–8	27	(75)
85:7–13	28	(77)
90:1–12	29	(84)
93:1–2, 5	30	(87)
95	31	(89)
96:1–6, 11–13	32	(92)
98:1–6	33	(95)
100 (Cleveland)	34	(97)
100 (Gelineau)	35	(98)
100 (Hopson)	36	(101)

103:1–2, 9–14	37	(103)
106:1–6, 19–23	38	(108)
111:1–4, 9–10	39	(111)
112	40	(112)
116	41	(115)
118:19–29 (Hopson)	42	(118)
118:14–17, 22–24 (Hallock)	43	(119)
118:1, 4–5, 14, 17, 24 (Berthier)	44	(120)
122:1–7	45	(126)
124	46	(128)
125	47	(129)
126 (Hopson)	48	(130)
126 (Gelineau)	49	(131)
130	50	(134)
131	51	(135)
133	52	(137)
136:1–18, 21–26	53	(139)
137	54	(140)
141	55	(144)
145:1–5, 8–9 (Hopson)	56	(147)
145:8–9, 18–19 (Old Scottish Chant)	57	(149)
146:5–10	58	(151)
147:12–15, 19–20	59	(154)
148	60	(155)
149	61	(156)
150	62	(157)

Canticles and Ancient Hymns

Canticle of Zechariah (Byzantine Chant)	63	(158)
Canticle of Zechariah (Hughes)	64	(160)
Canticle of Simeon	65	(166)
Hymn to Christ as Light (Isele)	66	(167)
Hymn to Christ as Light (Gregorian)	67	(169)
We Praise You, O God	68	(171)
Canticle of Hannah	69	(172)
Canticle from Lamentations	70	(179)
Canticle of Creation (Hopson)	71	(180)
Canticle of Creation (Murray)	72	(181)
A Canticle of Praise	73	(182)
A Canticle of Penitence	74	(183)
Canticle of the Redeemed	75	(184)
The Beatitudes	76	(188)
Christ Our Passover	77	(190)
The Lord's Prayer (Rimsky-Korsakov)	78	(192)
The Lord's Prayer (Plainsong Chant)	79	(193)
The Lord's Prayer (Source unknown)	80	(194)

PREFACE

This collection contains selected psalms and canticles from *The Psalter: Psalms and Canticles for Singing*, published by Westminster/John Knox Press, that may be easily sung by a choir. Most of the settings are for SATB voices; however, many unison selections may be sung not only by a cantor but by a choir as well. Refrains for the congregation to be reproduced in service bulletins are in the back of the complete version of *The Psalter: Psalms and Canticles for Singing*.

Ways to Use This Collection Effectively
Depending on the text and musical structure, most of the settings in this collection can be enhanced by the use of some of the following ideas:

- Some of the SATB settings may be sung without accompaniment.
- Verses may be alternated between cantor and choir.
- The SATB settings may be alternated between full choir and SATB quartet. (For some buildings the quartet can be placed in an antiphonal position.)
- The unison settings may be alternated between unison SA and TB voices.
- Children's voices may be used.
- The Gelineau psalm settings may be sung by either unison or SATB voices.
- The psalm refrain descants may be sung on the last one or two refrains.
- There are few dynamic markings; however, variance in dynamics can contribute greatly to the interpretation of some of the settings.
- Some of the longer psalms may be shortened by taking into consideration the text and its relationship to the other lectionary passages.
- Depending on many factors, the refrain may be sung less often or more often than is indicated. For example, the refrain to Jefferson Cleveland's Psalm 100 may be sung after every eight-measure phrase rather than just at the beginning and ending of the psalm.
- The choir should always be conscious of leading the congregation in singing the refrain.
- If the choir sings all the verses, it is helpful for a cantor or leader to cue the congregation in singing the refrain.

Specific Creative Ways to Use These Settings in Worship
- A psalm or canticle may be sung in lieu of the traditional organ prelude.
- Carefully chosen psalm and canticle refrains may be sung as effective calls to worship.
- Both the texts and music to many psalms and canticles provide valuable possibilities for anthems.
- Music during communion may be sung from the vast repertoire of selections in this volume.

PSALMS

PSALM 5
(1–8)

Hal H. Hopson

Hal H. Hopson
Tone to verses based on an Eastern Orthodox tone

REFRAIN

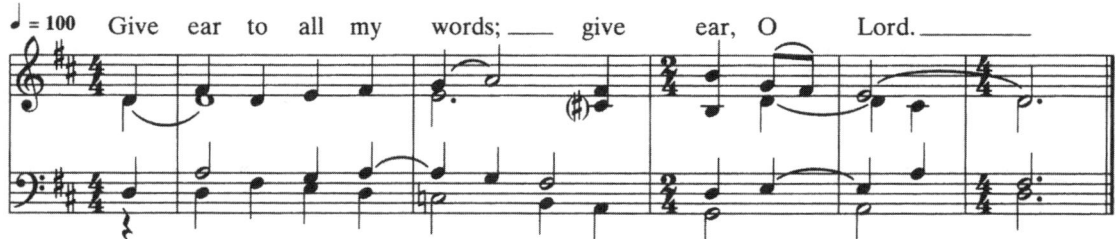

TONE

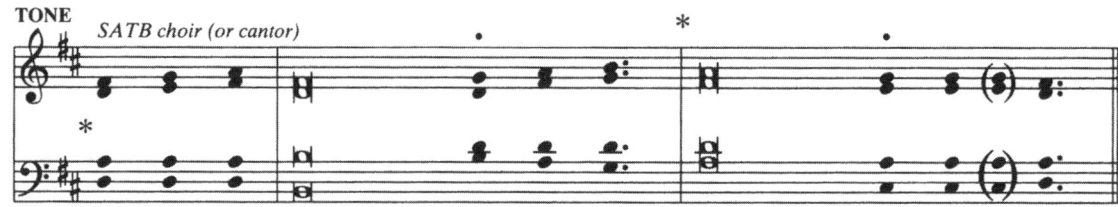

VERSES

1 *Give ear to* all my words, O Lord;*
  heed the sigh of my heart.

2 Listen, my voice cries out;*
  O God, to you I pray. **(R)**

3 *Lord, in the* morning you hear my voice;*
  in the morning I watch and pray.

4 You are not a God who delights in evil;*
  the wicked are not your guest. **(R)**

5 *Those who are* boastful shall not stand before your face;*
  you hate the ways of the evil.

6 You put aside those who do not speak the truth;*
  you despise violence and those who are full of deceit. **(R)**

7 *Through your great* love I come into your house;*
  in your temple I bow in awe.

8 Lord, lead me in your righteousness; my foes are near;*
  make clear my way ahead. **(R)**

*The italicized words are sung to these three notes of the intonation.

Text and music copyright 1985 by Hope Publishing Company, Carol Stream, IL 60188. All rights reserved.
Used by permission.

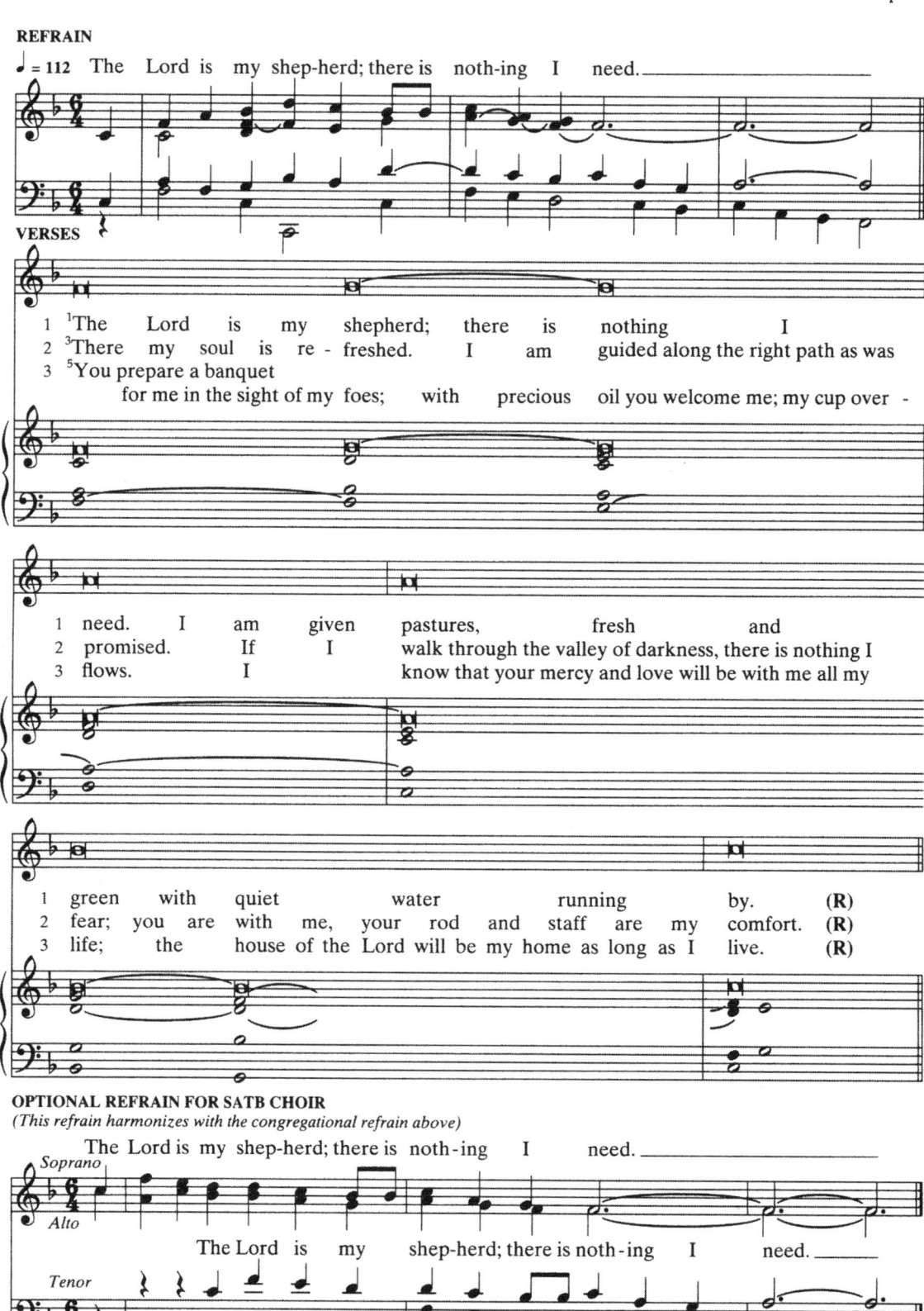

PSALM 24

5

Refrain: Willard F. Jabusch, alt.
Verses: Arlo D. Duba

Israeli Folk Melody
Arr: John Ferguson
Instrumentation: Kenneth E. Williams
and Lynelle M. Williams

REFRAIN (♩ = 108)

Lift up the gates e-ter-nal, lift up your voic-es;
the king of glo-ry comes, the na-tion re-joic-es.

VERSES

1. ¹See, all the earth is God's, its peo-ple and na-tions;
2. ³Who can go up this moun-tain, who stand in prais-ing?
3. ⁵They shall re-ceive for-give-ness, and have God's bless-ing
4. ⁷Come, lift your voic-es high, be lift-ed to glo-ry;
5. ⁸Who is this glo-rious one, for whom we are wait-ing?
6. ⁹Come, lift your heads with joy; come, lift up your tow-er;
7. ¹⁰Who is this King of glo-ry of whom we're sing-ing?

1. ²God built it on the deeps and laid its foun-da-tions. (R)
2. ⁴Those who are pure, who come with clean hands up-rais-ing. (R)
3. ⁶if they will search for God, their Sav-ior con-fess-ing. (R)
4. the Lord our God ap-proach-es, come, shout the sto-ry. (R)
5. We wait the might-y Lord, our God cel-e-brat-ing. (R)
6. the King of glo-ry comes in full might and pow-er. (R)
7. Our God, this Lord of hosts, the vic-tory is bring-ing. (R)

Gradually increasing tempo and changing to higher key(s) can heighten the sense of joy and power in this psalm.

Verses text copyright 1986 Arlo D. Duba. All rights reserved. Used by permission.
Refrain text copyright 1967, Rev. Willard F. Jabusch. Published by OCP. 5536 NE Hassalo, Portland, OR 97213. All rights reserved. Used with permission.
Music from *Sing to God* copyright 1984, United Church Press. Used by permission.

PSALM 27
(1–6)

7

Refrain: Taizé, alt.
Verses: Helen L. Wright

Refrain: Jacques Berthier (Taizé)
Tone: Hal H. Hopson
Refrain harm.: Hal H. Hopson

REFRAIN

TONE *SATB choir (or cantor)*

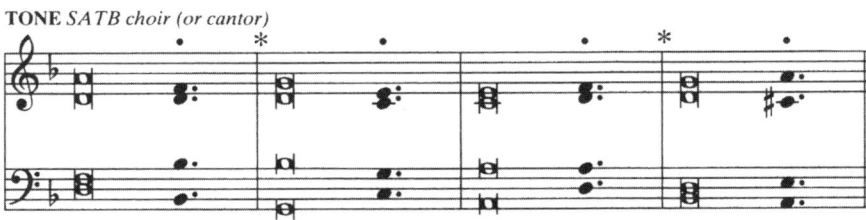

VERSES

1. ¹The Lord is my light and my salvation*
   whom shall I fear?
   The Lord is the stronghold of my life,*
   of whom shall I be afraid? **(R)**

2. ²When evil ones draw near to devour my flesh,*
   they are the ones who waver and fall.
   ³Though an army camp against me, my heart will not fear;*
   though war rage against me, my trust will still be firm. **(R)**

3. ⁴One thing I ask of the Lord, one thing I seek;*
   to live in the house of God all the days of my life,
   to behold the beauty of the Lord and to pray in the temple;*
   ⁵for in the day of trouble I am safe, hidden in the tent of God. **(R)**

4. The Lord will keep me secure,*
   setting me firmly on a rock.
   ⁶Now my head is held up high*
   above my foes who surround me. **(R)**

5. Within God's tent I offer thanks,*
   a sacrifice of joy.
   I will sing a psalm of praise to the Lord,*
   I will make melody to God. **(R)**

*Optional choir counter melody

The Lord is my light, my light and sal-va-tion; in God I trust, in God I trust.

The refrain may be sung in the traditional manner by the congregation, and the counter melody may be added, sung by the choir. As an extended introduction or coda, the choir may sing the refrain and counter melody together, repeating several times.

Text copyright 1984 Helen L. Wright. All rights reserved. Used by permission.
Verses music copyright 1986 by Hope Publishing Company, Carol Stream, IL 60188. All rights reserved. Used by permission.
Refrain copyright 1982, Ateliers et Presses de Taizé, Taizé Community, France. GIA Publications, Inc., exclusive North American agent, 7404 S. Mason Ave., Chicago, IL 60638. www.giamusic.com. 800.442.1358. All rights reserved. Used by permission.

PSALM 30
(1–2, 4–5, 11–12)

8

Hal H. Hopson

Refrain: Hal H. Hopson
Tone: William Byrd

REFRAIN

♩ = 132 Sing praise to the Lord. Sing praise to the Lord, all the earth.

VERSES

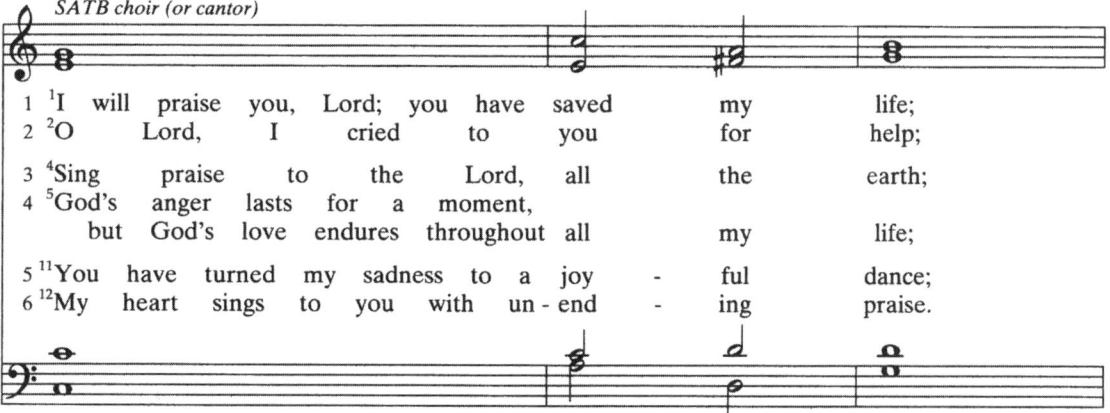

SATB choir (or cantor)

1 ¹I will praise you, Lord; you have saved my life;
2 ²O Lord, I cried to you for help;
3 ⁴Sing praise to the Lord, all the earth;
4 ⁵God's anger lasts for a moment,
   but God's love endures throughout all my life;
5 ¹¹You have turned my sadness to a joy - ful dance;
6 ¹²My heart sings to you with un - end - ing praise.

1 you have not let my foes tri - umph o - ver me.
2 you healed me, you kept me from the grave. **(R)**
3 give thanks and bless God's ho - ly name.
4 tears may flow in the night, but joy comes with the dawn. **(R)**
5 you have taken away my sorrow;
   I am clothed with glad - ness all the day.
6 O Lord, I will give you thanks for ev - er - more. **(R)**

Text and refrain copyright 1985 by Hope Publishing Company, Carol Stream, IL 60188.
All rights reserved. Used by permission.

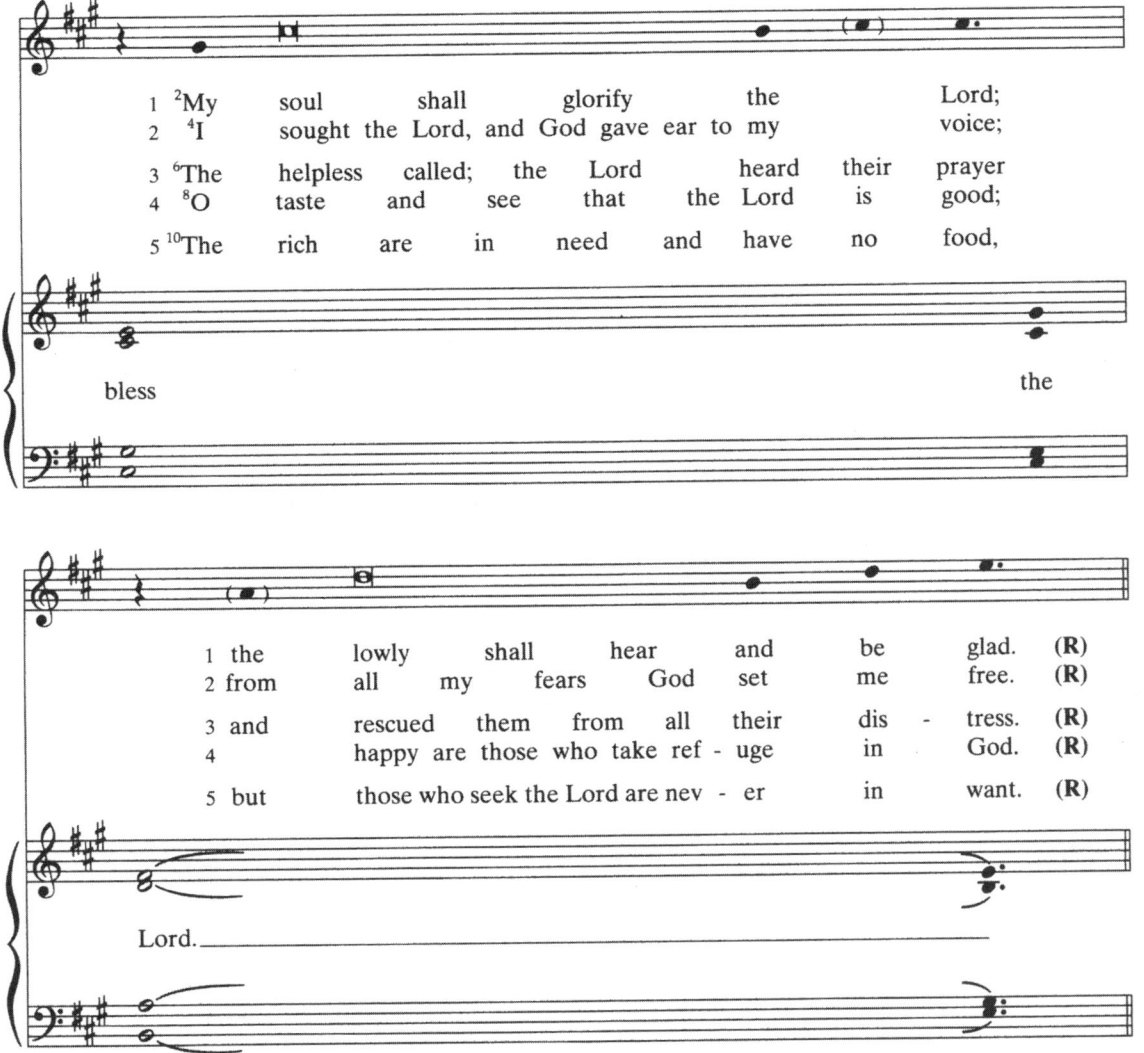

Text and music copyright 1989 by Hope Publishing Company, Carol Stream, IL 60188.
All rights reserved. Used by permission.

PSALM 36
(5–11)

The Grail

Refrain: David Clark Isele
Tone: Joseph Gelineau

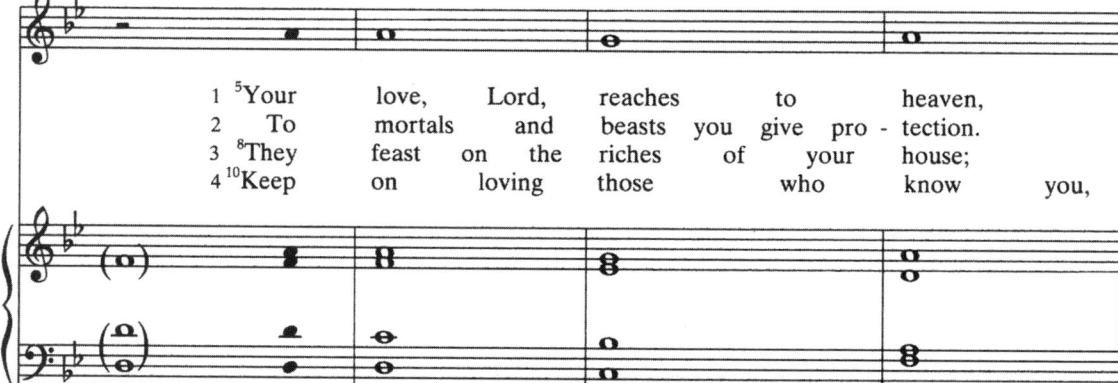

1 ⁵Your love, Lord, reaches to heaven,
2 To mortals and beasts you give protection.
3 ⁸They feast on the riches of your house;
4 ¹⁰Keep on loving those who know you,

1 your truth to the skies.
2 ⁷O Lord, how precious is your love.
3 they drink from the stream of your delight.
4 doing justice for upright hearts.

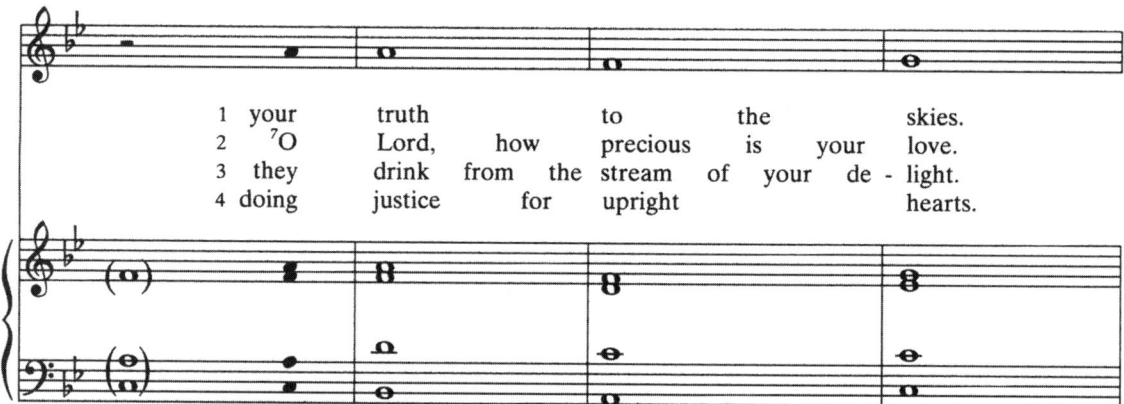

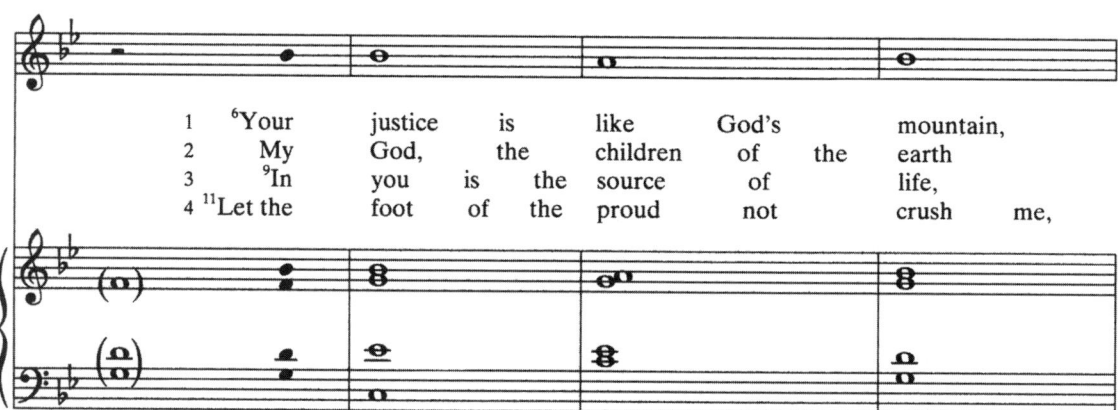

1 ⁶Your justice is like God's mountain,
2 My God, the children of the earth
3 ⁹In you is the source of life,
4 ¹¹Let the foot of the proud not crush me,

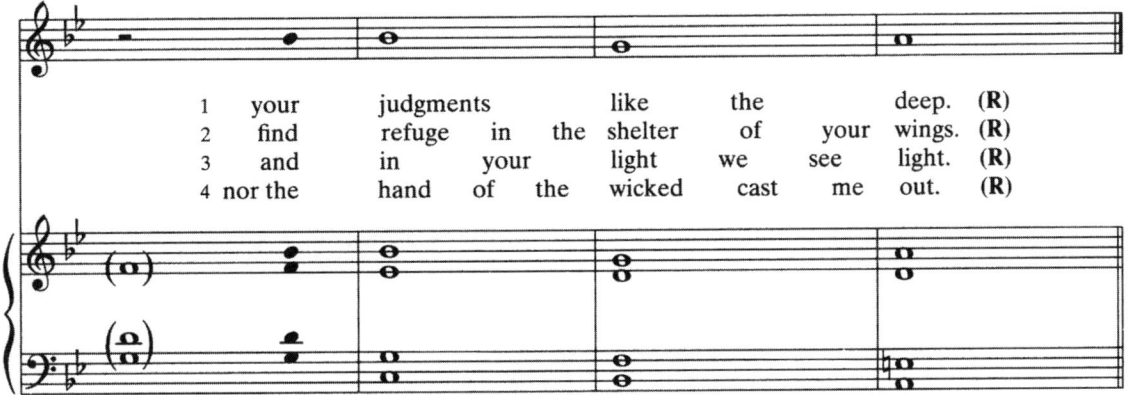

11   PSALM 42

The Grail, alt.

Refrain: Joseph Gelineau
Tone: Frederick A. Gore Ouseley

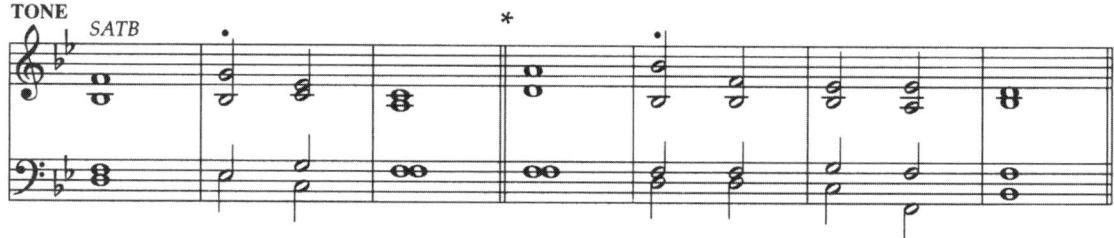

REFRAIN: My soul is thirsting for the Lord; when shall I see God face to face?

VERSES

1. ¹Like the deer that yearns for running streams,*
   so my soul is yearning for you, my God.

   ²My soul is thirsting for God, the God of my life,*
   when can I enter and see the face of God?

   ³My tears have become my bread, by night, by day,*
   as I hear it said all the day long: "Where is your God?" **(R)**

2. ⁴These things will I remember as I pour out my soul:*
   how I would lead the rejoicing crowd into the house of God,
   amid cries of gladness and thanksgiving,*
   the throng wild with joy?

   ⁵Why are you cast down, my soul, why groan within me?*
   Hope in God, whom again I praise, my savior ⁶and my God.

   My soul is cast down within me as I think of you,*
   from the country of Jordan and Mount Hermon, from the Hill
   of Mizar. **(R)**

3. ⁷Deep is calling on deep, in the roar of waters;*
   your torrents and all your waves swept over me.

   ⁸By day the Lord will send loving kindness;*
   by night I will sing praise to the God of my life.

   ⁹I will say to God, my rock: "Why have you forgotten me?*
   Why do I go mourning oppressed by the foe?"

   ¹⁰With cries that pierce me to the heart, my enemies revile me,*
   saying to me all the day long: "Where is your God?"

   ¹¹Why are you cast down, my soul, why groan within me?*
   Hope in God, whom again I praise, my savior and my God. **(R)**

The ⌢ connects two syllables to be sung to one chord.
The •• identifies one syllable to be sung to two chords.

Verses text and refrain © 1963, 1986 The Grail, England, GIA Publications, Inc., exclusive North American agent, 7404 S. Mason Ave., Chicago, IL 60638. www.giamusic.com. 800.442.1358. All rights reserved. Used by permission.

PSALM 43

Refrain: Joseph Gelineau
Tone: Frederick A. Gore Ouseley

The Grail, alt.

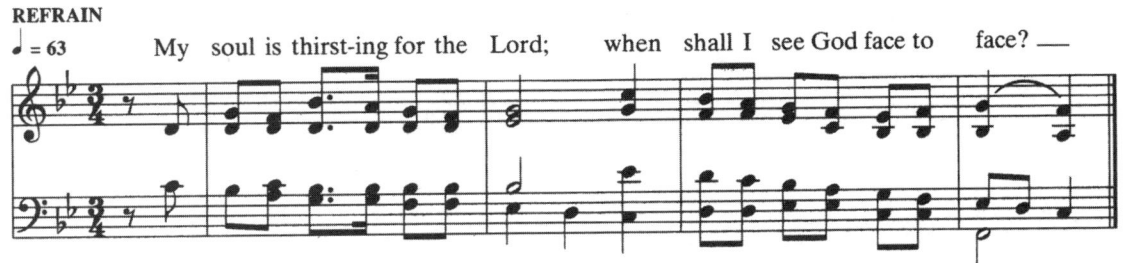

VERSES

1. Defend me, O God, and plead my cause against a godless nation.*
   From a deceitful and cunning people rescue me, O God.

2. Since you, O God, are my stronghold, why have you rejected me?*
   Why do I go mourning, oppressed by the foe? **(R)**

3. O send forth your light and your truth; let these be my guide.*
   Let them bring me to your holy mountain, to the place
      where you dwell.

4. And I will come to your altar, O God, the God of my joy.*
   My redeemer, I will thank you on the harp, O God, my God.

5. Why are you cast down, my soul, why groan within me?*
   Hope in God, whom again I praise, my savior and my God. **(R)**

The ⌒ connects two syllables to be sung to one chord.
The •• identifies one syllable to be sung to two chords.

Verses text and refrain © 1963, 1986 The Grail, England, GIA Publications, Inc., exclusive North American agent, 7404 S. Mason Ave., Chicago, IL 60638. www.giamusic.com. 800.442.1358. All rights reserved. Used by permission.

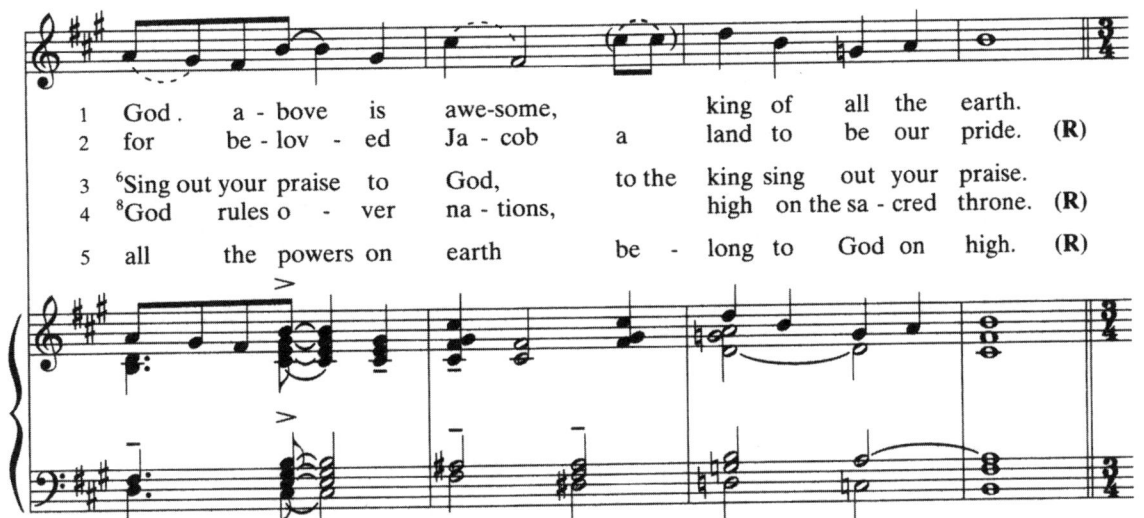

Text and music from *Psalms for All Seasons* copyright 1987, International Committee on English in the Liturgy (ICEL). All rights reserved.

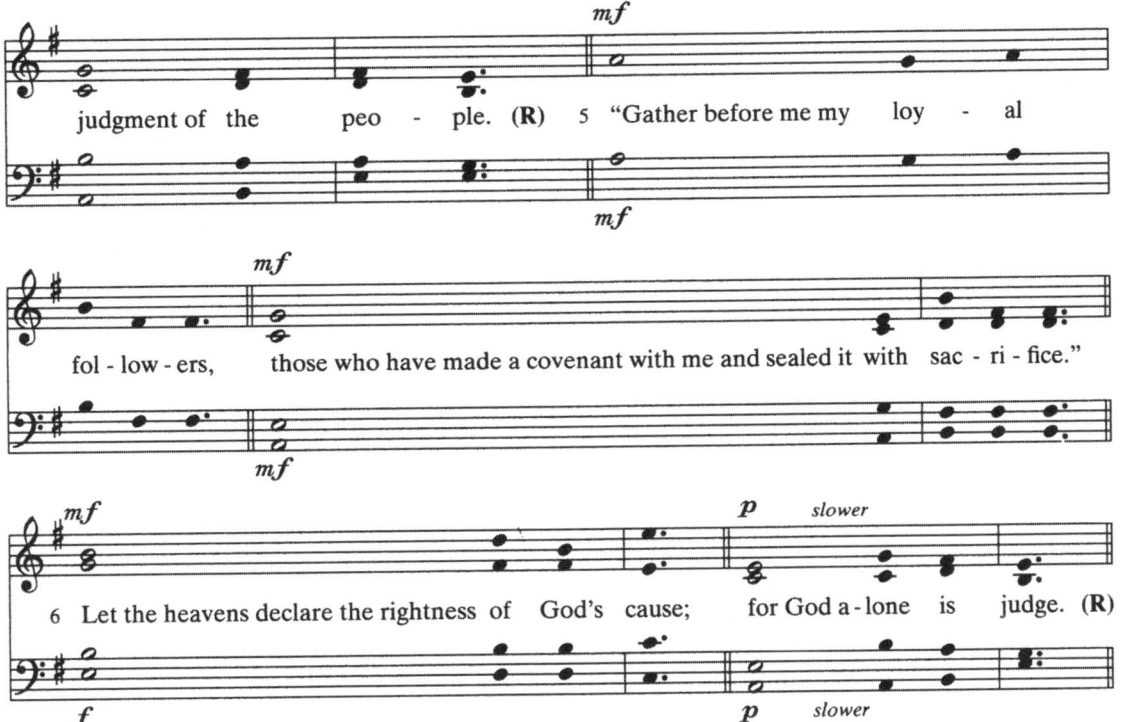

Music copyright 1986 by Ionian Arts, Inc.

15 PSALM 51
(1–12)

Book of Common Prayer Peter R. Hallock

*Note: The Second Soprano and Baritone parts are optional; if performed in four parts, Altos should sing the Second Soprano part.

Music copyright 1987 by Ionian Arts, Inc.

PSALM 62
(5–12)

16

Refrain: Robert Batastini
Tone: Source unknown

A New Zealand Prayer Book/He Karakia Mihinare o Aotearoa

REFRAIN

TONE *SATB choir (or cantor)*

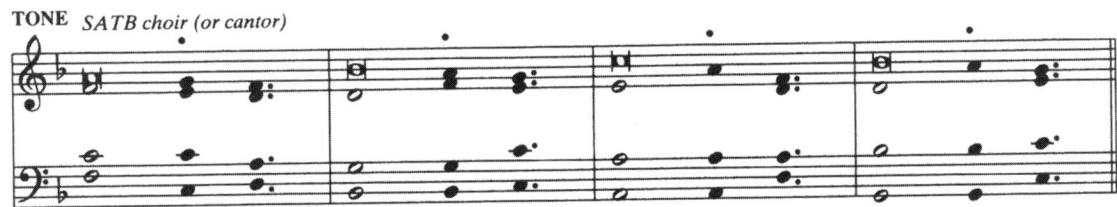

VERSES

1 ⁵Yet be still, my soul, and wait for God:
  from whom comes my hope of deliverance.
  ⁶God only is my rock and my salvation:
  my tower of strength, so that I stand unshaken. **(R)**

2 ⁷In God is my deliverance and my honor:
  the rock of my strength and my place of refuge.
  ⁸Put your trust in God always, you people:
  pour out your hearts before the one who is our refuge. **(R)**

3 ⁹For we mortals are only a puff of wind;
  the great among us are but illusion:
  weighed in the balance they rise upward,
  all of them lighter than air. **(R)**

4 ¹⁰Put no trust in extortion,
  set no vain hopes on plunder:
  if riches increase,
  do not set your heart upon them. **(R)**

5 ¹¹Once God has spoken, and twice I have heard God say:
  "Power belongs to God alone."
  ¹²Steadfast love, O Lord, is yours:
  and you reward us all according to our deeds. **(R)**

Refrain © 1975 by GIA Publications, Inc., 7404 S. Mason Ave., Chicago, IL 60638.
www.giamusic.com. 800.442.1358. All rights reserved. Used by permission.
Verses text copyright 1989   The Provincial Secretary, The Church in the Province of New Zealand.

PSALM 63
(1–8)

Arlo D. Duba

Refrain: Presbyterian 8
Tone: Thomas Tallis

REFRAIN

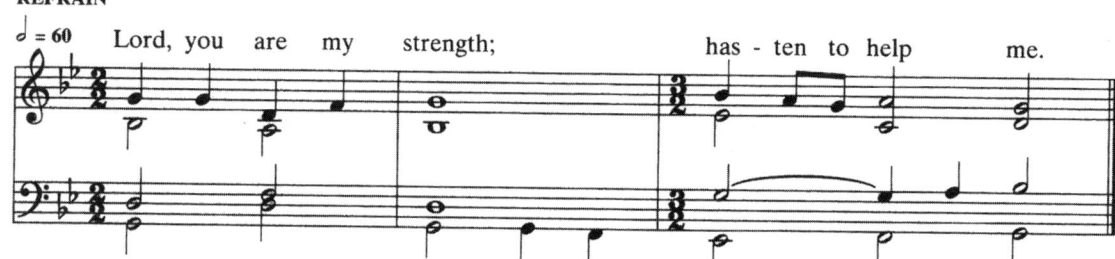

Lord, you are my strength; hasten to help me.

VERSES *SATB choir*

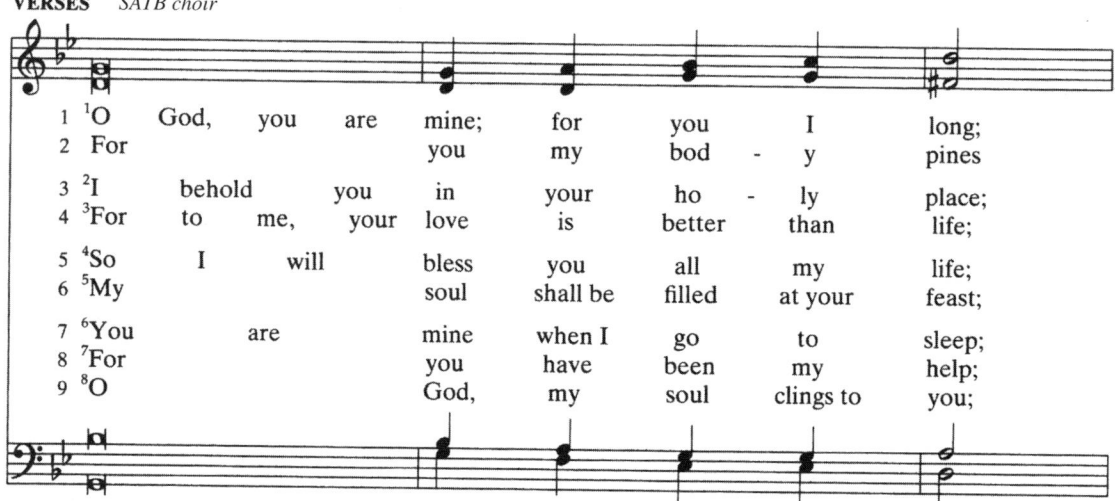

1 ¹O God, you are mine; for you I long;
2 For you my body pines
3 ²I behold you in your holy place;
4 ³For to me, your love is better than life;
5 ⁴So I will bless you all my life;
6 ⁵My soul shall be filled at your feast;
7 ⁶You are mine when I go to sleep;
8 ⁷For you have been my help;
9 ⁸O God, my soul clings to you;

1 for you my soul is a-thirst.
2 like a dry, weary land where all water is gone. **(R)**
3 there I see your glory and your power.
4 thus, my lips will sing out your praise. **(R)**
5 I will lift up my hands in your name.
6 my mouth shall praise you with joy. **(R)**
7 you re-main with me all through the night.
8 in the shadow of your wings I re-joice.
9 your right hand will still hold me fast. **(R)**

Verses text copyright 1986 Arlo D. Duba. All rights reserved. Used by permission.
Verses music copyright 1987 The Westminster Press.
Refrain copyright 1986 by Hope Publishing Company, Carol Stream, IL 60188. All rights reserved. Used by permission.

Text and music copyright 1988 by Hope Publishing Company, Carol Stream, IL 60188. All rights reserved. Used by permission.

19 PSALM 67

Hal H. Hopson

Refrain: Hal H. Hopson
Tone: Gregorian VI f

REFRAIN

Let the peo-ple praise you, O God; let all the peo-ple praise you.

VERSES

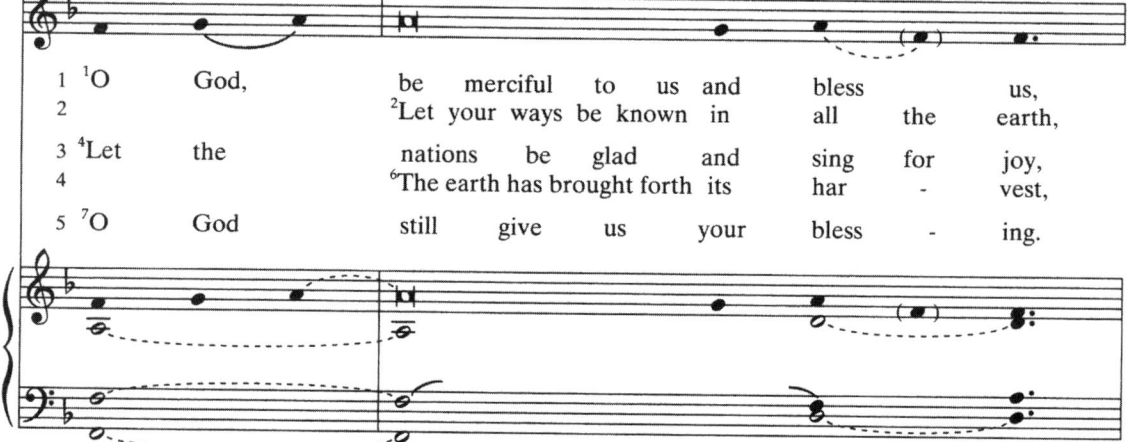

1 ¹O God, be merciful to us and bless us,
2 ²Let your ways be known in all the earth,
3 ⁴Let the nations be glad and sing for joy,
4 ⁶The earth has brought forth its har - vest,
5 ⁷O God still give us your bless - ing.

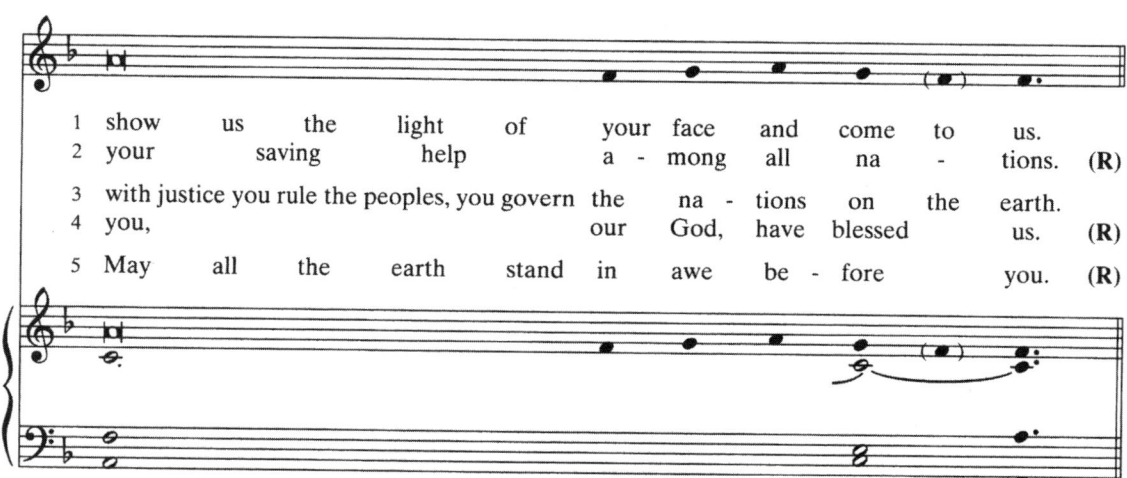

1 show us the light of your face and come to us.
2 your saving help a - mong all na - tions. **(R)**
3 with justice you rule the peoples, you govern the na - tions on the earth.
4 you, our God, have blessed us. **(R)**
5 May all the earth stand in awe be - fore you. **(R)**

Text and refrain copyright 1988 by Hope Publishing Company, Carol Stream, IL 60188. All rights reserved. Used by permission.

PSALM 67

Hal H. Hopson

Hal H. Hopson
Tone to verses based on an Eastern Orthodox tone

REFRAIN

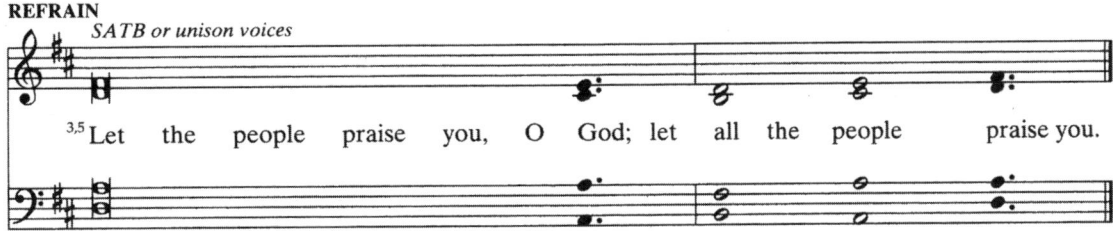

3,5 Let the people praise you, O God; let all the people praise you.

VERSES

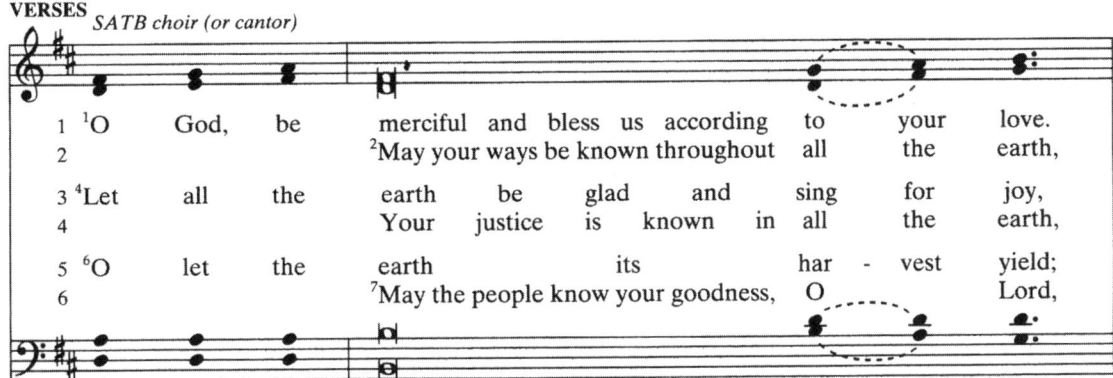

1 ¹O God, be merciful and bless us according to your love.
2 ²May your ways be known throughout all the earth,
3 ⁴Let all the earth be glad and sing for joy,
4 Your justice is known in all the earth,
5 ⁶O let the earth its har-vest yield;
6 ⁷May the people know your goodness, O Lord,

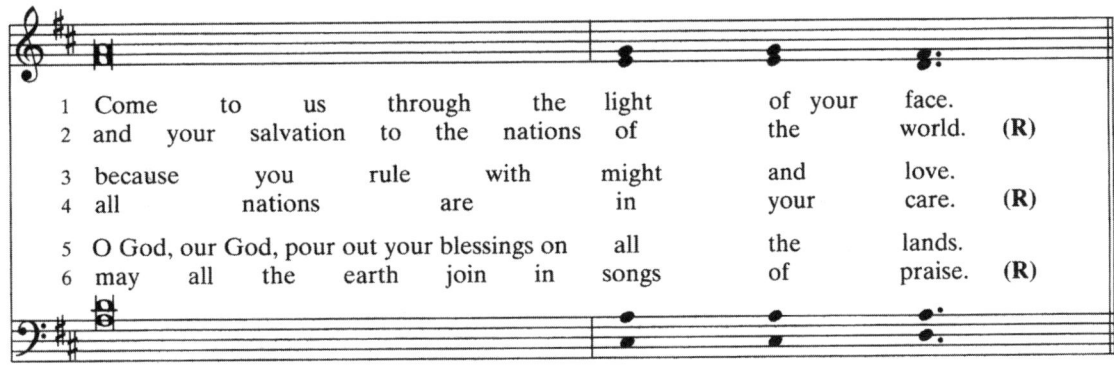

1 Come to us through the light of your face.
2 and your salvation to the nations of the world. (R)
3 because you rule with might and love.
4 all nations are in your care. (R)
5 O God, our God, pour out your blessings on all the lands.
6 may all the earth join in songs of praise. (R)

Text and music copyright 1988 by Hope Publishing Company, Carol Stream, IL 60188. All rights reserved. Used by permission.

PSALM 70

Book of Common Prayer
Peter R. Hallock

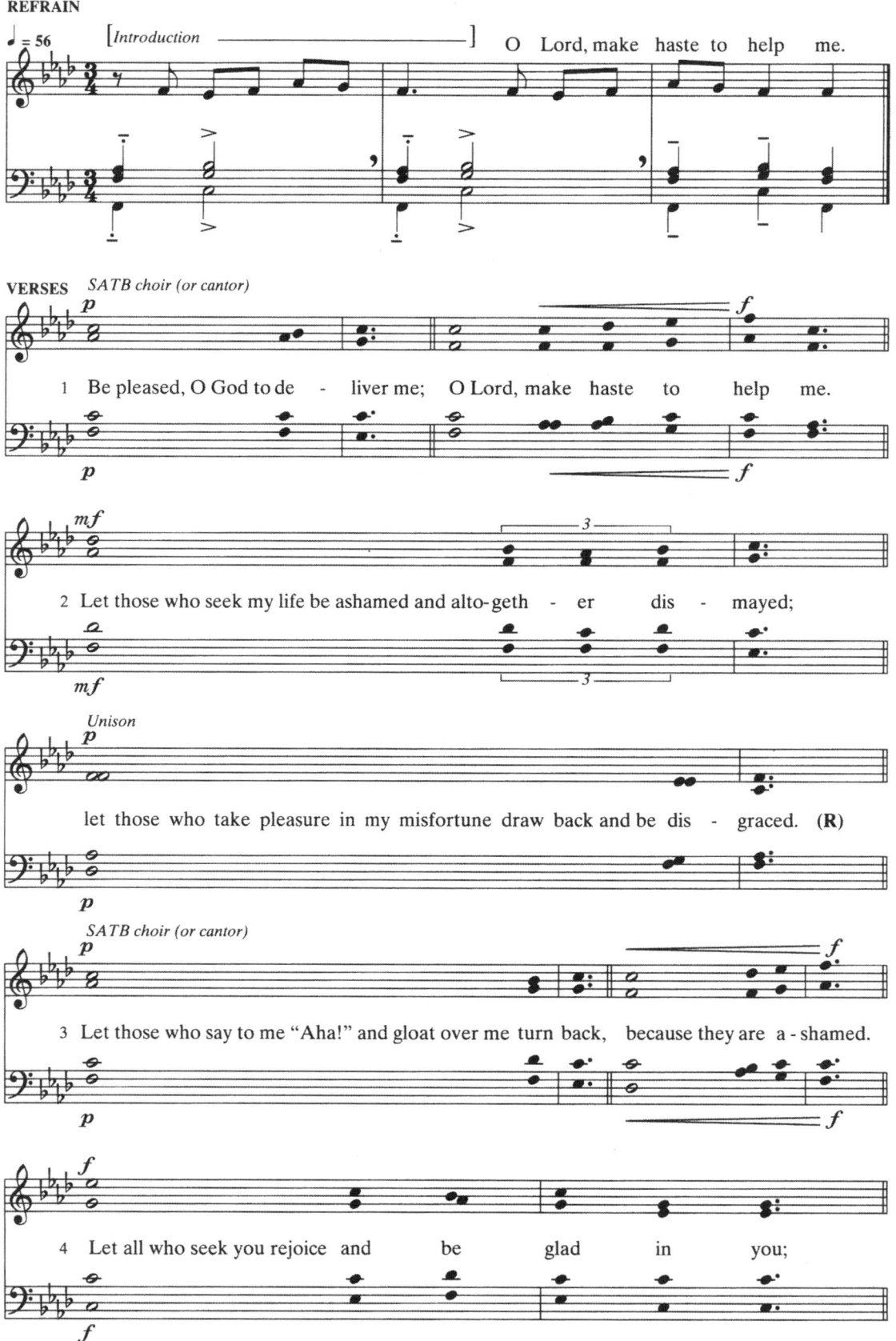

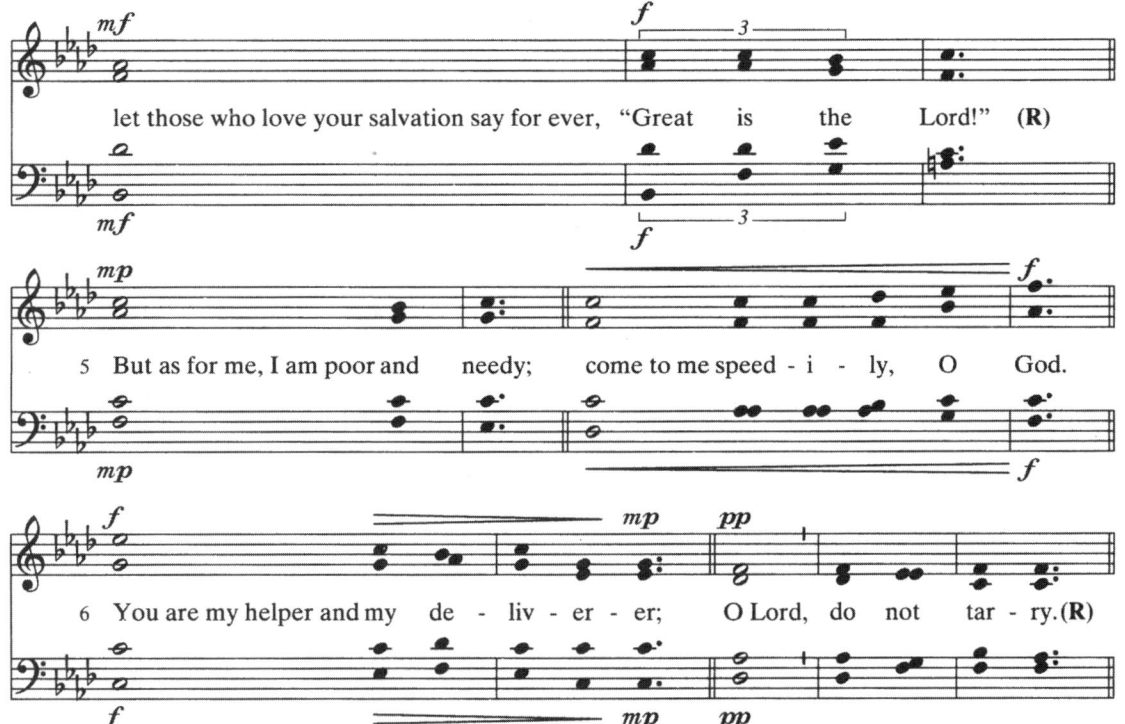

Music copyright 1987 by Ionian Arts, Inc.

22 PSALM 72
(Advent 1–8, 17–19)
(Epiphany 1–8, 10, 12–13)

Book of Common Prayer, alt. Peter R. Hallock

Music copyright 1986 by Ionian Arts, Inc.

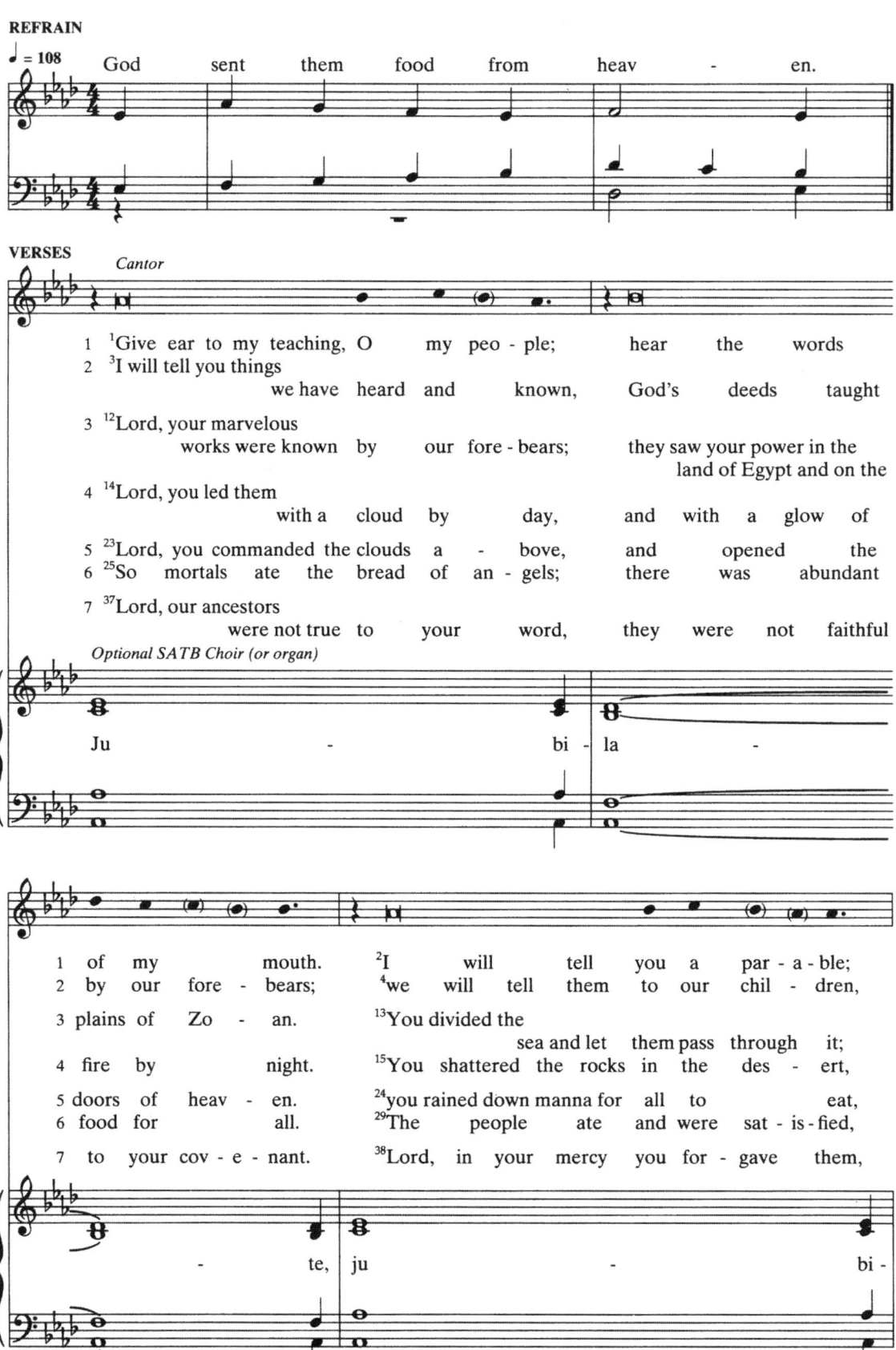

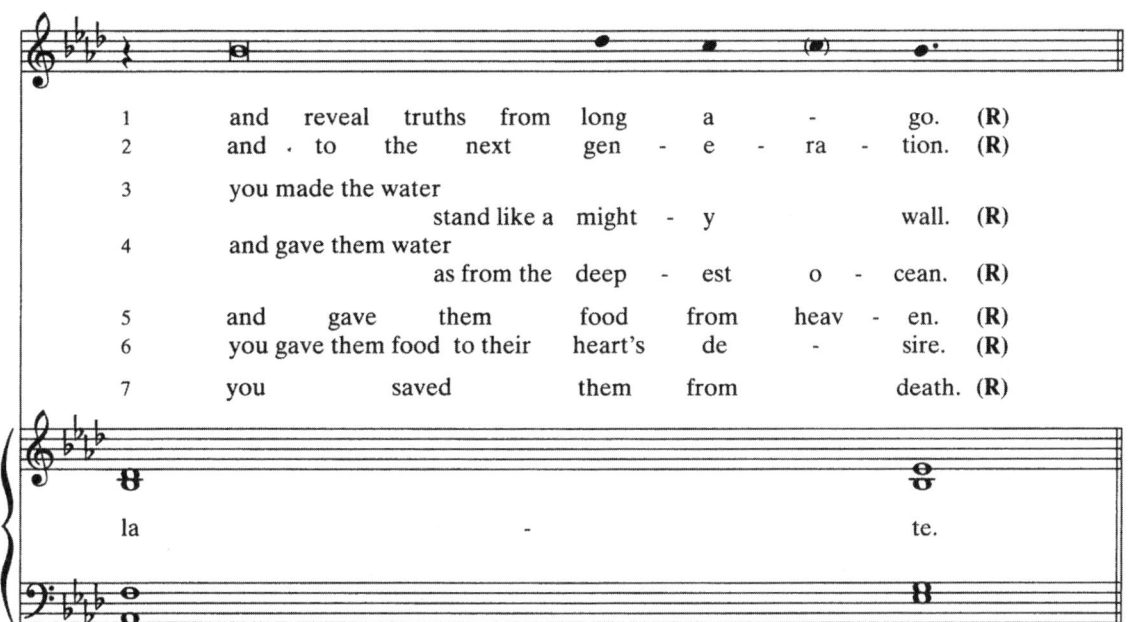

1	and reveal truths from long a - go. **(R)**
2	and · to the next gen - e - ra - tion. **(R)**
3	you made the water stand like a might - y wall. **(R)**
4	and gave them water as from the deep - est o - cean. **(R)**
5	and gave them food from heav - en. **(R)**
6	you gave them food to their heart's de - sire. **(R)**
7	you saved them from death. **(R)**

la - te.

Text and music copyright 1989 by Hope Publishing Company, Carol Stream, IL 60188. All rights reserved. Used by permission.

24 PSALM 79
(1–9)

The Grail

Refrain: Howard Hughes, S.M.
Tone: Joseph Gelineau

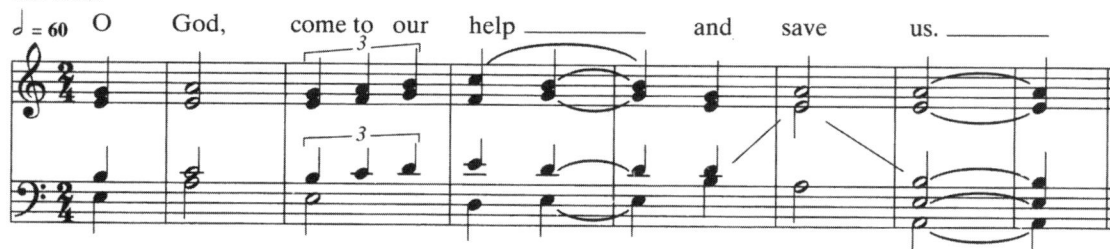

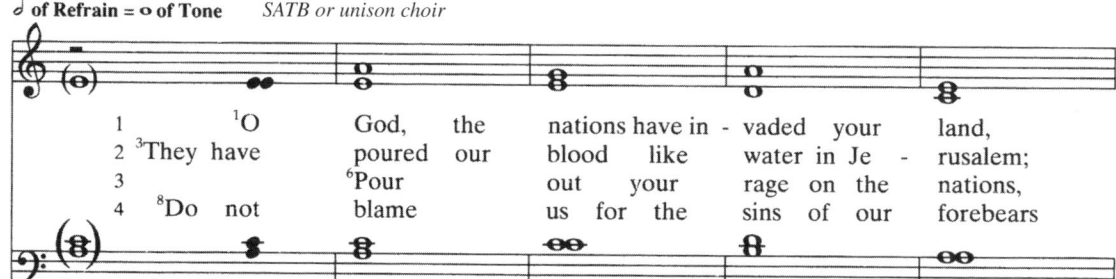

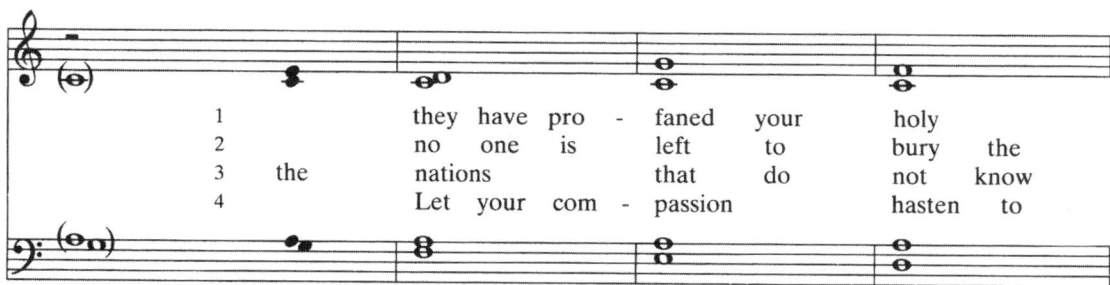

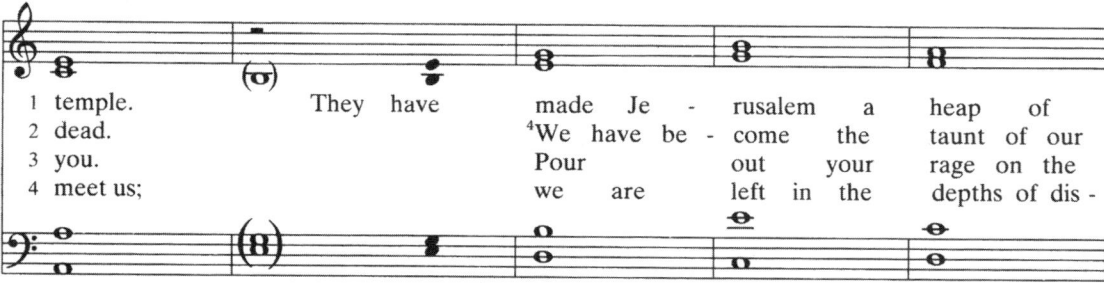

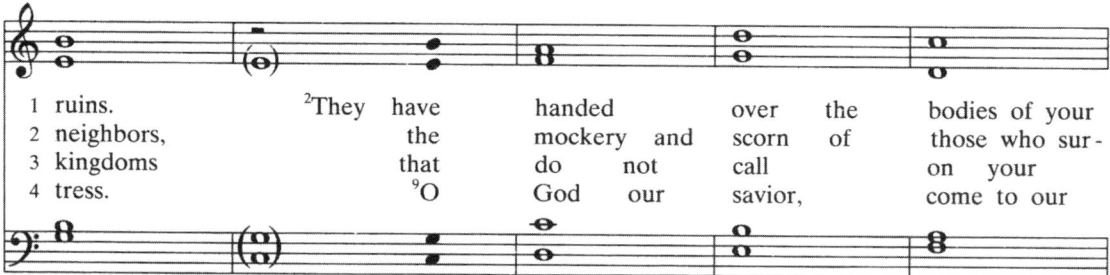

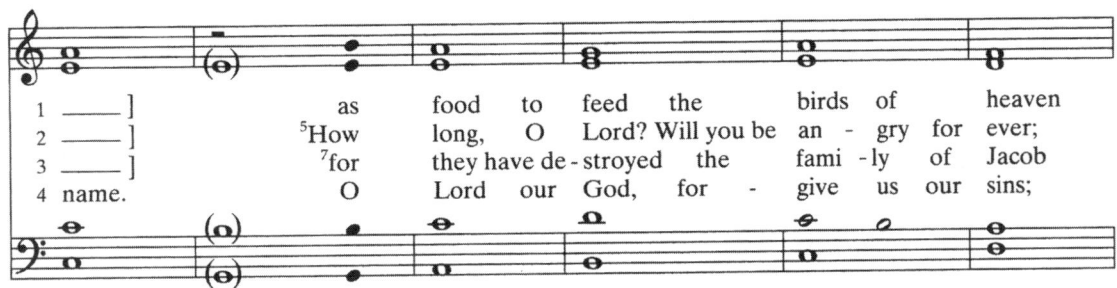
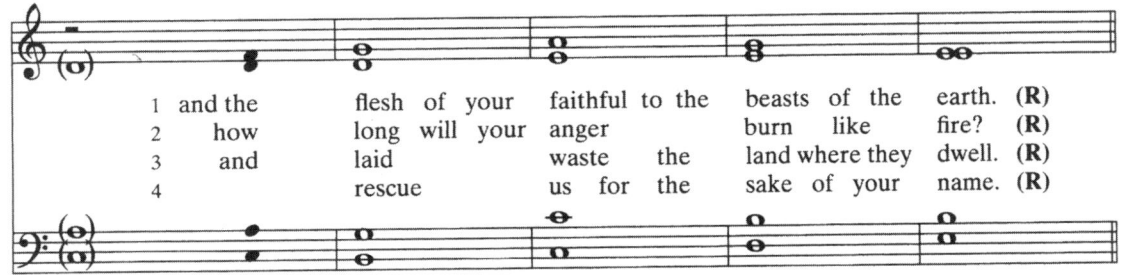

Verses text and music © 1963, 1986 The Grail, England, GIA Publications, Inc., exclusive North American agent, 7404 S. Mason Ave., Chicago, IL 60638. www.giamusic.com. 800.442.1358. All rights reserved. Used by permission.
Refrain copyright 1991 by Howard Hughes, S.M.

PSALM 82

26

Book of Common Prayer, alt.

Refrain: Howard Hughes, S.M.
Tone: Gregorian IVa
Harmonization: Kenneth E. Williams

REFRAIN

A-rise, O God; a-rise and rule the earth.

VERSES *Choir unison*

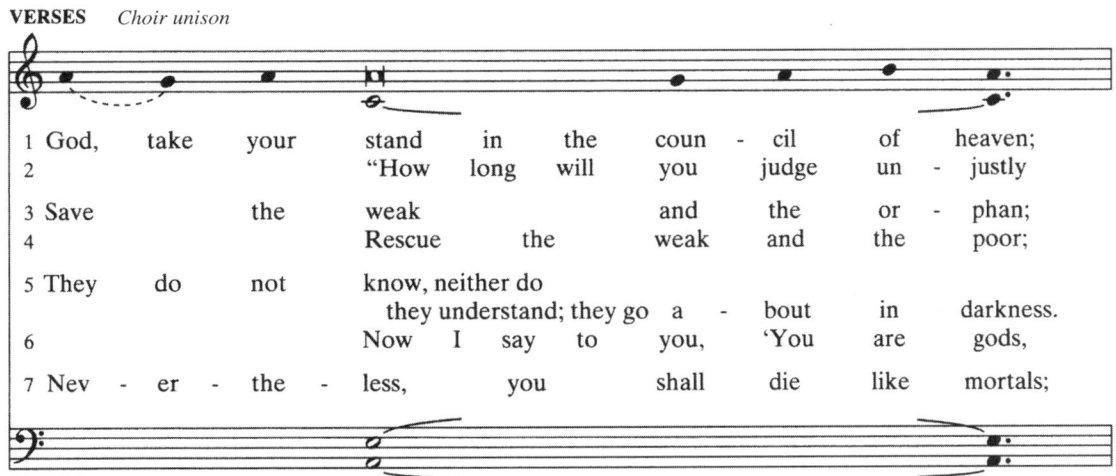

1 God, take your stand in the coun-cil of heaven;
2 "How long will you judge un-justly
3 Save the weak and the or-phan;
4 Rescue the weak and the poor;
5 They do not know, neither do they understand; they go a-bout in darkness.
6 Now I say to you, 'You are gods,
7 Nev-er-the-less, you shall die like mortals;

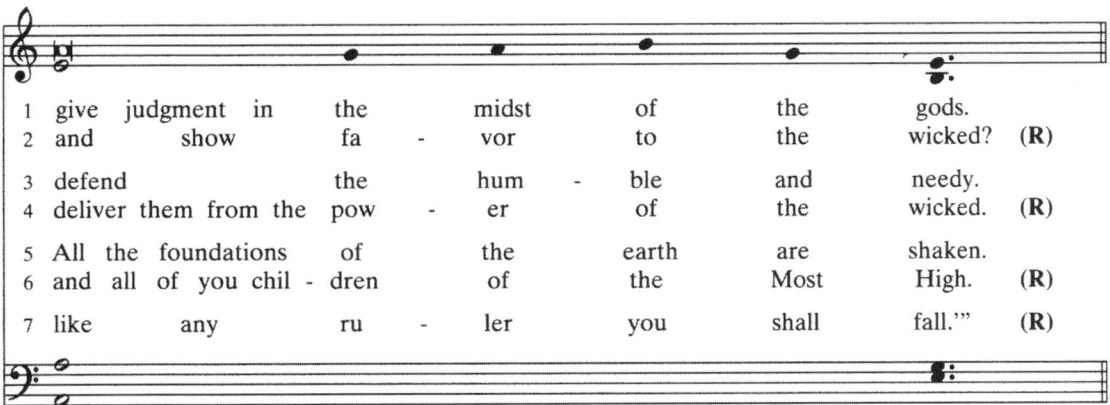

1 give judgment in the midst of the gods.
2 and show fa-vor to the wicked? **(R)**
3 defend the hum-ble and needy.
4 deliver them from the pow-er of the wicked. **(R)**
5 All the foundations of the earth are shaken.
6 and all of you chil-dren of the Most High. **(R)**
7 like any ru-ler you shall fall.'" **(R)**

Optional Descant

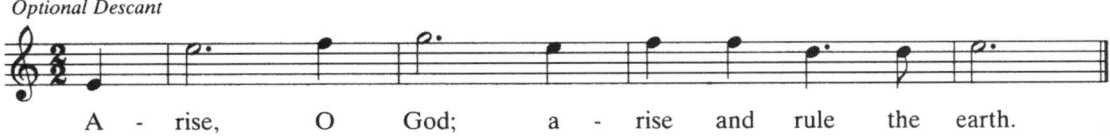
A-rise, O God; a-rise and rule the earth.

Refrain music copyright 1991 by Howard Hughes, S.M.
Harmonization of tone copyright 1989 by Kenneth E. Williams.

PSALM 84
(1–8)

Hal H. Hopson

Copyright 1989 by Hope Publishing Company, Carol Stream, IL, 60188. All rights reserved. Used by permission.

29 PSALM 90
(1–12)

Hal H. Hopson

Refrain and Tone A: Hal H. Hopson
Tone B: Based on Eastern Orthodox Tone

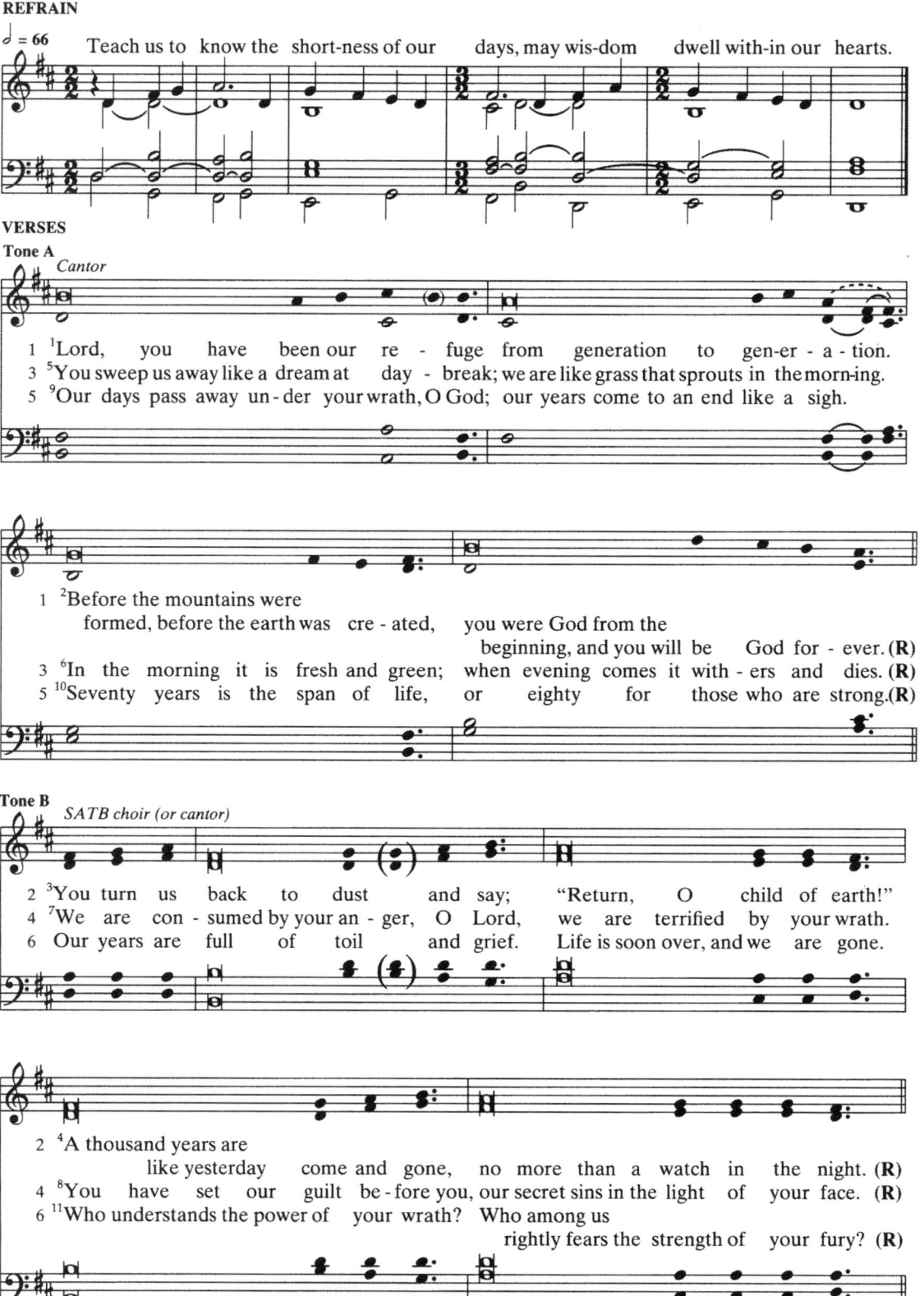

Copyright 1988 by Hope Publishing Company, Carol Stream, IL 60188. All rights reserved. Used by permission.

PSALM 93
(1–2, 5)

Refrain: International Commission on English in the Liturgy
Verses: *New American Bible*

J. Gerald Phillips

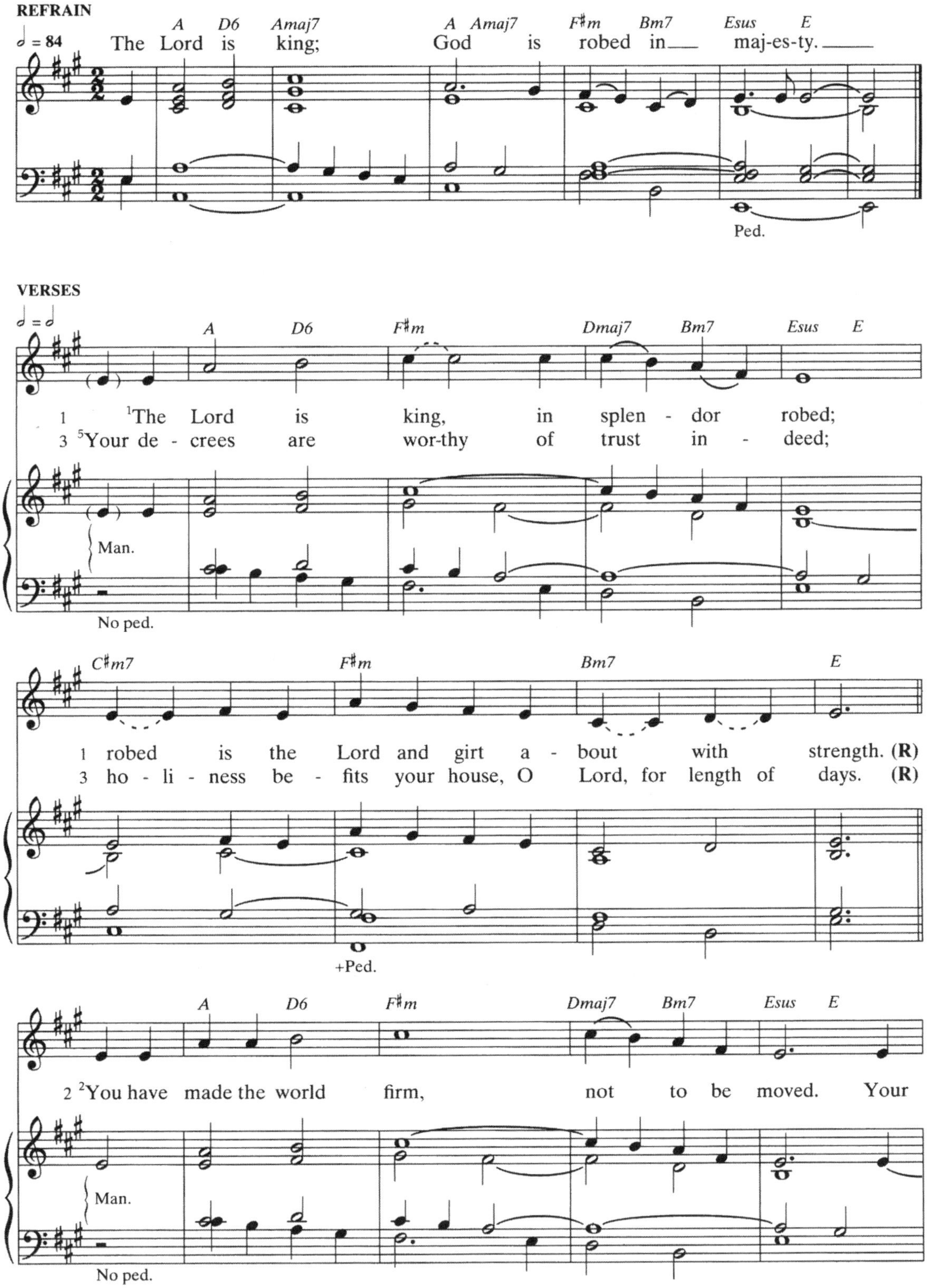

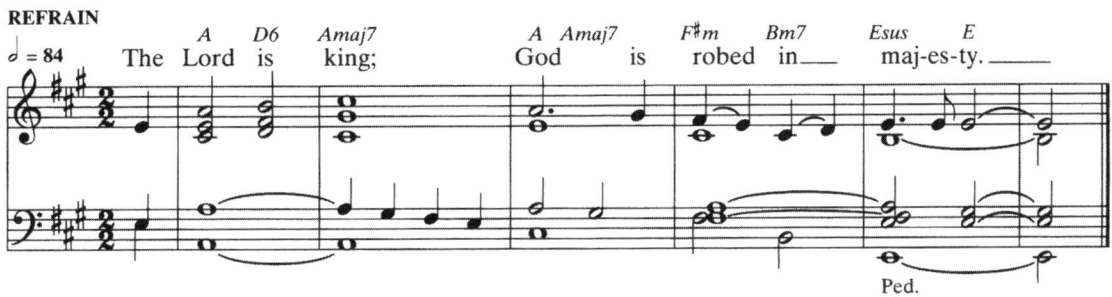

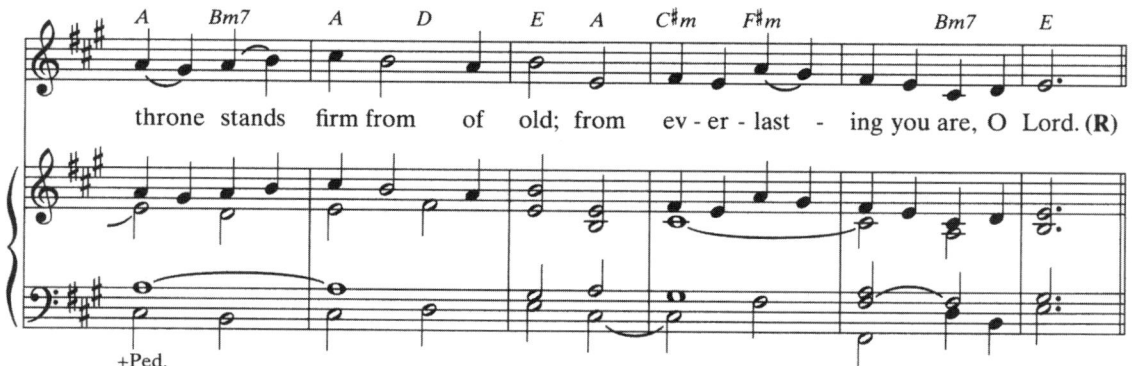

Music copyright 1984, World Library Publications, Franklin Park, IL. www.wlpmusic.com. All rights reserved. Used by permission.
Verses text from the *New American Bible* copyright 1970 by the Confraternity of Christian Doctrine, Washington, D.C. Used by permission.
Refrain text from the *Lectionary for Mass* ©1969, International Committee on English in the Liturgy, Inc. (ICEL). All rights reserved.

PSALM 95

New Church Hymnal, alt.
William Boyce

Text verses 1–4 by William Boyce, from *The New Church Hymnal* copyright 1937, 1965 and published by Fleming H. Revell, a division of Baker Publishing Group.
Verses 5–6: Source unknown.

PSALM 98
(1–6)

33

Book of Common Prayer, alt.

Peter R. Hallock

Music copyright 1986 by Ionian Arts, Inc.

PSALM 100

34

J. Jefferson Cleveland
J. Jefferson Cleveland

REFRAIN
En-ter God's gates with thanks and praise.

VERSES
1. Shout to the Lord, all the land; 2. serve the Lord with joy; come be-fore God with laugh-ter. 3. Know that the Lord is God; we be-long to the Lord our ma-ker, to God, who tends us like sheep. 4. Come to God's gates with thanks; come to God's courts with praise;

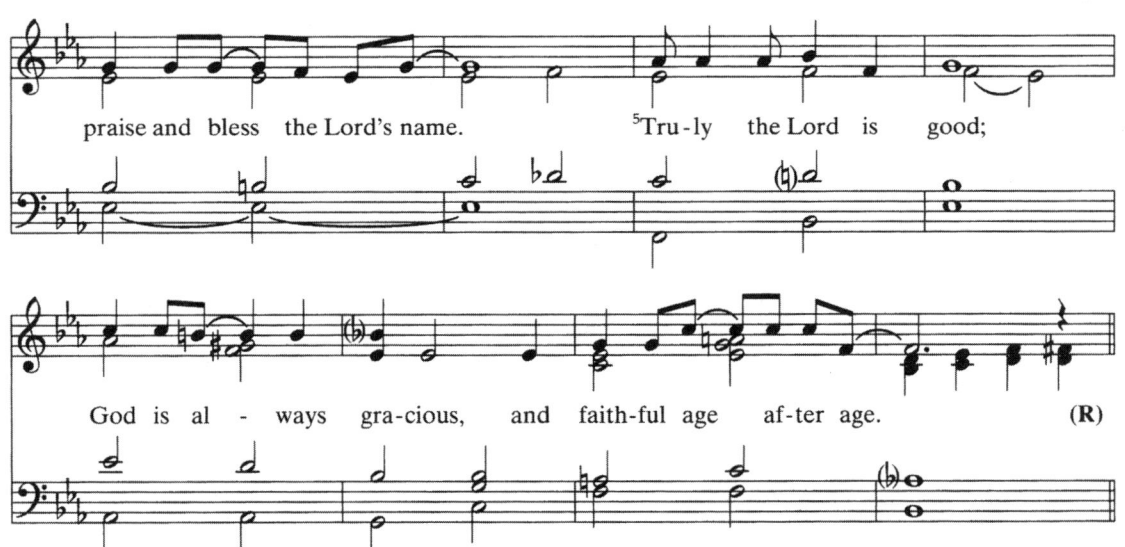

Copyright 1984 The Upper Room.

PSALM 100

The Grail Joseph Gelineau

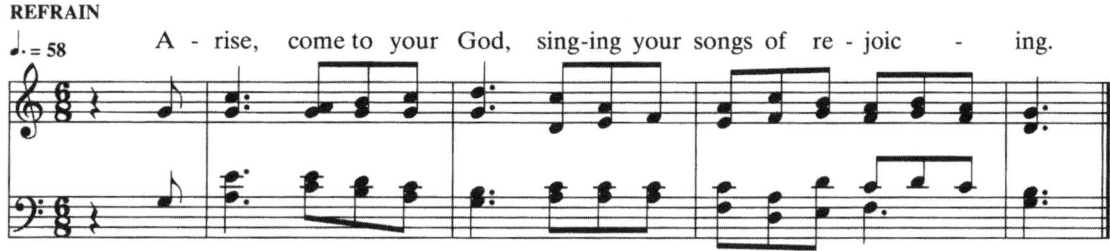

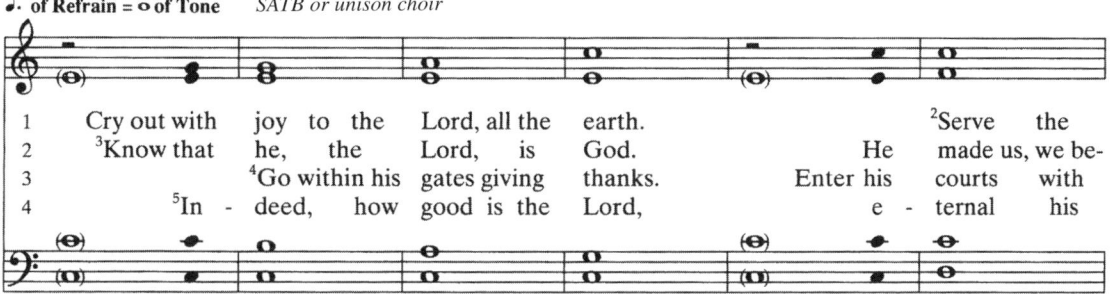

Text and music © 1963, 1986 The Grail, England, GIA Publications, Inc., exclusive North American agent, 7404 S. Mason Ave., Chicago, IL 60638. www.giamusic.com. 800.442.1358. All rights reserved. Used by permission.

OSTINATO (to accompany the verses)

DESCANT FOR REFRAIN

PERFORMANCE SUGGESTIONS

The harmony of the four measures of the refrain and of the verses is compatible on each beat. Depending on the resources of each situation, a variety of creative possibilities exists by making use of the various optional parts. The refrain may be used as a four-part canon. Sung by various combinations of cantor, choir(s), and congregation, Psalm 100 may be sung as: (1) a call to worship, (2) a response to a scripture reading, (3) an anthem sung by one or more choirs, (4) and as an informal fellowship song with the refrain sung as a four-part canon for gatherings such as church dinners.

Copyright 1988 by Hope Publishing Company, Carol Stream, IL 60188. All rights reserved. Used by permission.

37 PSALM 103
(1–2, 9–14)

The United Methodist Liturgical Psalter Peter R. Hallock

Music copyright 1987 by Ionian Arts, Inc.
Text: *The United Methodist Liturgical Psalter*, edited by Harrell Beck, John Holbert, S.T. Kimbrough, Jr., and Alan Luff.   Copyright 1989   The United Methodist Publishing House. (Administered by the Copyright Company, Nashville, TN). All rights reserved. International copyright secured. Used by permission. Based on the *New Revised Standard Version Bible*, 1989, and adapted by permission of the Division of Christian Education of the National Council of Churches of Christ in the U.S.A.

38 PSALM 106
(1–6, 19–23)

A New Zealand Prayer Book/He Karakia Mihinare o Aotearoa

Hal H. Hopson

VERSES

1 ¹Praise the Lord. O give thanks, for the Lord is good:*
God's love endures forever.

²Who can recount your mighty acts, O Lord,*
or tell of all your praise? **(R)**

2 ³Blessed are those who act justly*
and always do what is right.

⁴Remember me, Lord, when you show favor to your people,*
and come to me with your saving help,

⁵so that I may see the prosperity of your chosen:*
rejoice with the nation's gladness,

and exult with the people*
you have made your own. **(R)**

3 ⁶We have sinned like our ancestors;*
we have erred, and we have acted wickedly.

¹⁹They made a young bull in Horeb*
and worshipped that molten image.

²⁰So they exchanged the glory of God*
for the image of a creature that feeds on grass. **(R)**

4 ²¹They forgot that you were the God who had saved them*
by your mighty acts in Egypt,

²²wonderful things in the land of Ham,*
and awesome things at the Red Sea.

²³So you would have destroyed them but for Moses, your chosen one,*
who stood before you in the breach, to turn back your wrath from their destruction. **(R)**

Verses text copyright 1989 The Provincial Secretary, The Church in the Province of New Zealand.
Verses music and refrain copyright 1988 by Hope Publishing Company, Carol Stream, IL 60188. All rights reserved. Used by permission.

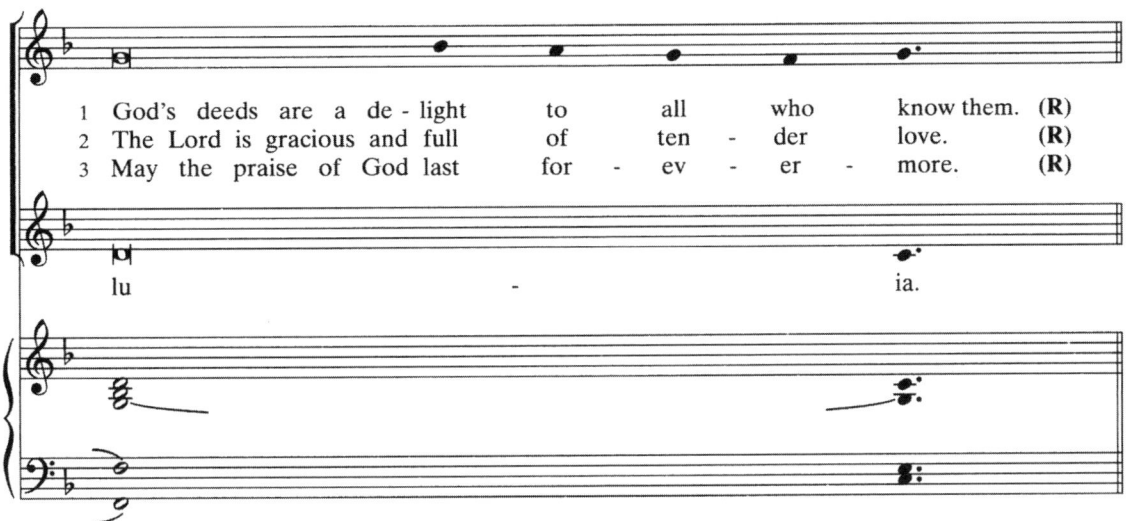

1 God's deeds are a de-light to all who know them. (R)
2 The Lord is gracious and full of ten - der love. (R)
3 May the praise of God last for - ev - er - more. (R)

lu - ia.

* *The countermelody may be sung by a single solo voice, a treble ensemble, or all treble voices.*

Copyright 1989 by Hope Publishing Company, Carol Stream, IL 60188. All rights reserved. Used by permission.

PSALM 116

41

Helen L. Wright

Refrain: Richard Proulx
Tone: Saint Meinrad 1

REFRAIN

TONE *Choir unison*

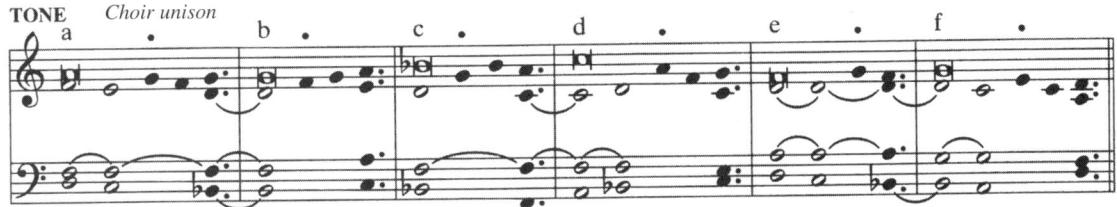

VERSES

1. ¹I love the Lord who has heard my prayer,
   ²who bends down to hear my call.

   ³The cords of death entangled me;
   the grip of the grave took hold of me.

   ⁴Then I called on the name of the Lord,
   "I beg you, save my soul!" **(R)**

2. ⁵Our Lord is gracious and just,
   our God is merciful.

   ⁶The Lord watches over the helpless;
   I was brought low, but God helped me.

   ⁷Be at rest again, my heart,
   for the Lord has blessed you with many gifts. **(R)**

3. a ⁸God has delivered me from death, *(go to f)*
   f my eyes from tears, my feet from stumbling.

   ⁹I will walk in the presence of the Lord
   in the land of the living.

   ¹⁰I have faith even when I say,
   "I am wholly crushed;"

   ¹¹even when in my alarm
   I say, "None can be trusted." **(R)**

4. ¹²How can I repay the Lord
   for the goodness done for me?

   ¹³The cup of salvation I raise,
   and call on the name of the Lord.

   ¹⁴To the Lord I will pay my vows
   before all the people. **(R)**

5. ¹⁵How precious the death of the saints,
   those who remain faithful to God!

   ¹⁶Lord God, I am your slave,
   the child of a faithful mother.

   You have loosed my bonds,
   you have set me free. **(R)**

6. ¹⁷A sacrifice of thanks I bring
   and call on your name.

   ¹⁸To the Lord I will pay my vows
   before all the people.

   ¹⁹I will pay my vows to the Lord
   in the courts of God.

   In the midst of Jerusalem,
   Alleluia! **(R)**

OPTIONAL DESCANT

Text copyright 1991 Helen L. Wright. All rights reserved. Used by permission.
Refrain copyright 1977 by Richard Proulx.
Verses music copyright 1992 Saint Meinrad Archabbey.

42 PSALM 118
(19–29)

Hal H. Hospon
Hal H. Hopson

REFRAIN ♩ = 138

Choir (or cantor): Fling wide the gates!
Congregation: Fling wide the gates!
Choir (or cantor): Welcome the king!
Congregation: Welcome the king!

VERSES

Unison (Cantor or choir)

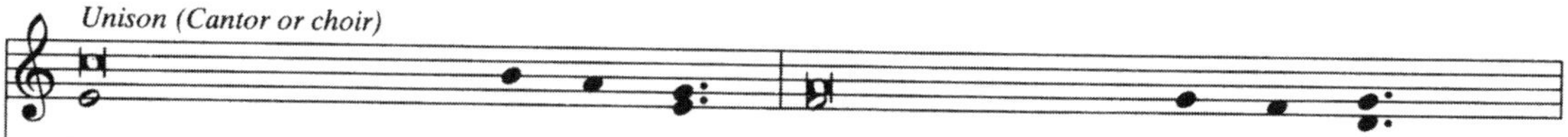

1. ¹⁹Let the doors of righteousness be opened; we will go in and give thanks to the Lord.
2. ²²The stone which the builders rejected as worthless has become the cornerstone.
3. ²⁵Send salvation, O Lord; Lord, grant us victory.
4. [————————————————————————]

SATB or unison choir (or cantor)

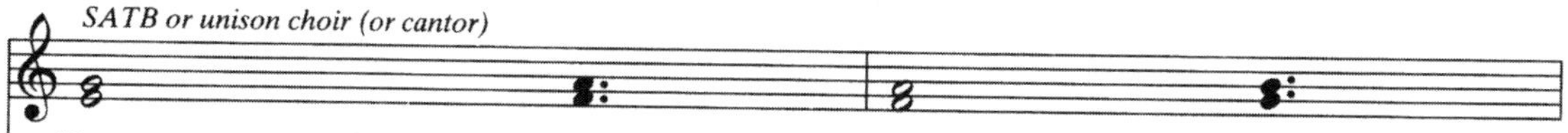

1. ²⁰This is the gate of the Lord; it is opened for the righteous.
2. ²³This is your work, O Lord, a marvel in our eyes.
3. ²⁶Blessed be your name, O Lord. We bless you from your temple.
4. ²⁸You are our God; we give you praise; we will proclaim your greatness.

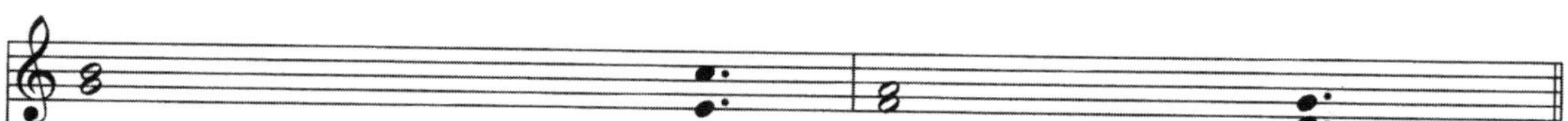

1. ²¹We will give praise, for God has heard us and has come to save us. **(R)**
2. ²⁴Lord, you have made this day; let us rejoice and be glad. **(R)**
3. ²⁷Lord God, you have given us light; with waving branches we march around the altar. **(R)**
4. ²⁹We will offer thanks because of your goodness; your love endures forever. **(R)**

Copyright 1989 by Hope Publishing Company, Carol Stream, IL 60188. All rights reserved. Used by permission.

PSALM 118
(14–17, 22–24)

Book of Common Prayer

Peter R. Hallock

43

* The bass part may be sung an octave lower throughout where there are cue notes.

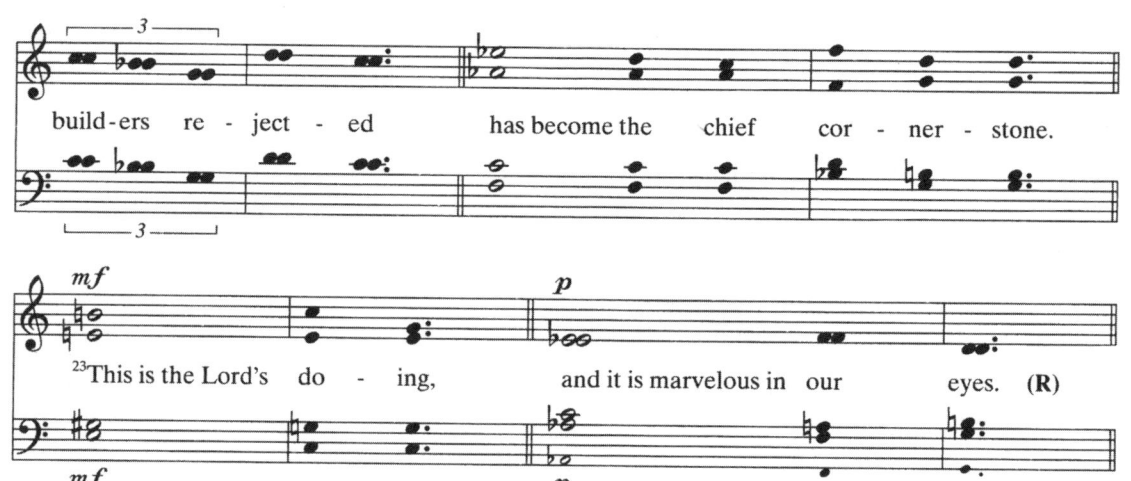

Music copyright 1986 by Ionian Arts, Inc.

PSALM 118
(1, 4–5, 14, 17, 24)

44

Taizé, alt.
Jacques Berthier (Taizé)

Copyright 1982, Ateliers et Presses de Taizé, Taizé Community, France, GIA Publications, Inc., exclusive North American agent, 7404 S. Mason Ave., Chicago, IL 60638. www.giamusic.com. 800.442.1358. All rights reserved. Used by permission.

PSALM 122
(1–7)

The Grail

Refrain: Hal H. Hopson
Tone: Joseph Gelineau

REFRAIN

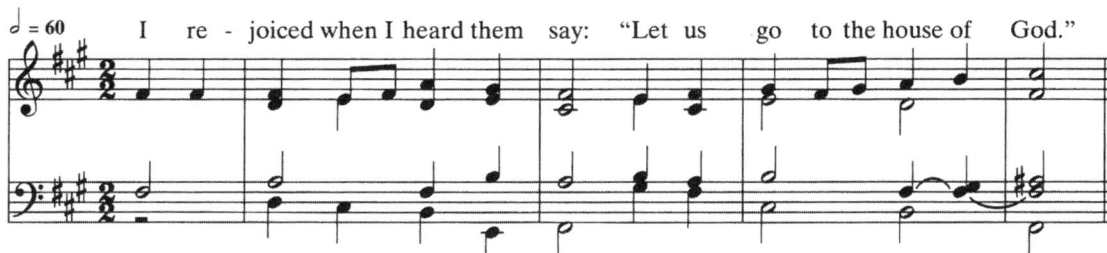

VERSES

𝅗𝅥 of Refrain = 𝅝 of Tone   SATB or unison choir

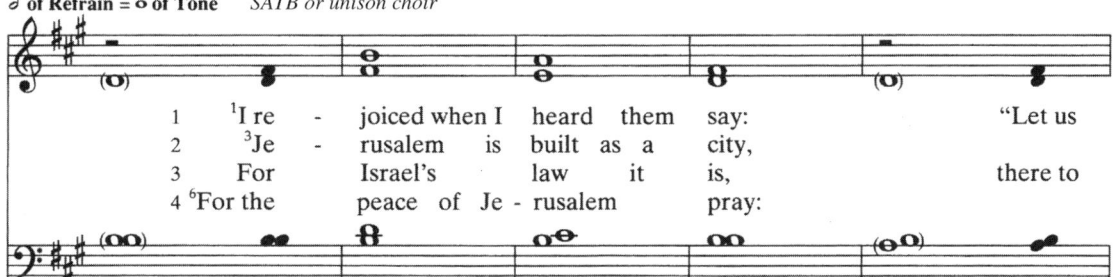

1 ¹I re - joiced when I heard them say: "Let us
2 ³Je - rusalem is built as a city,
3 For Israel's law it is,   there to
4 ⁶For the peace of Je - rusalem   pray:

1 go to God's house."   ²And now our feet are
2 strongly com - pact.   ⁴It is there that the tribes go
3 praise the Lord's name.   ⁵There were set the thrones of
4 "Peace be to your homes!   ⁷May peace reign in your

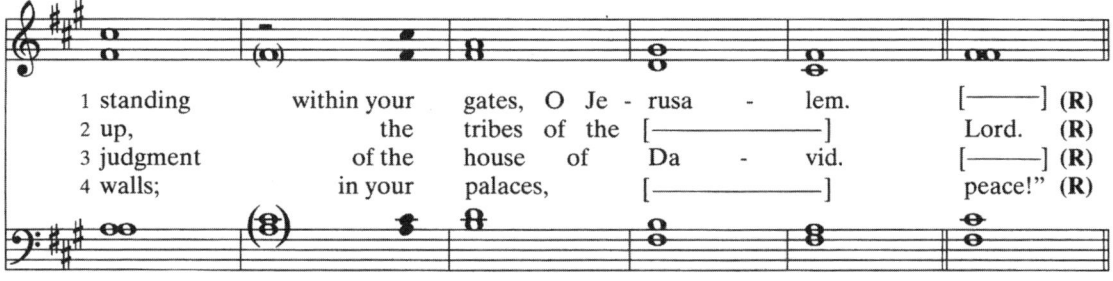

1 standing   within your gates, O Je - rusa - lem. [———] (R)
2 up,   the   tribes of the [————]   Lord.   (R)
3 judgment   of the   house of Da - vid.   [———] (R)
4 walls;   in your   palaces, [————]   peace!" (R)

Verses text and music copyright 1963, 1986 The Grail, England, GIA Publications, Inc., exclusive North American agent, 7404 S. Mason Ave., Chicago, IL 60638. www.giamusic.com. 800.442.1358. All rights reserved. Used by permission.
Refrain copyright 1982 by Hope Publishing Company, Carol Stream, IL 60188. All rights reserved. Used by permission.

Music copyright 1987 by Ionian Arts, Inc.
Text copyright 1984 Helen L. Wright. All rights reserved. Used by permission.

47   PSALM 125

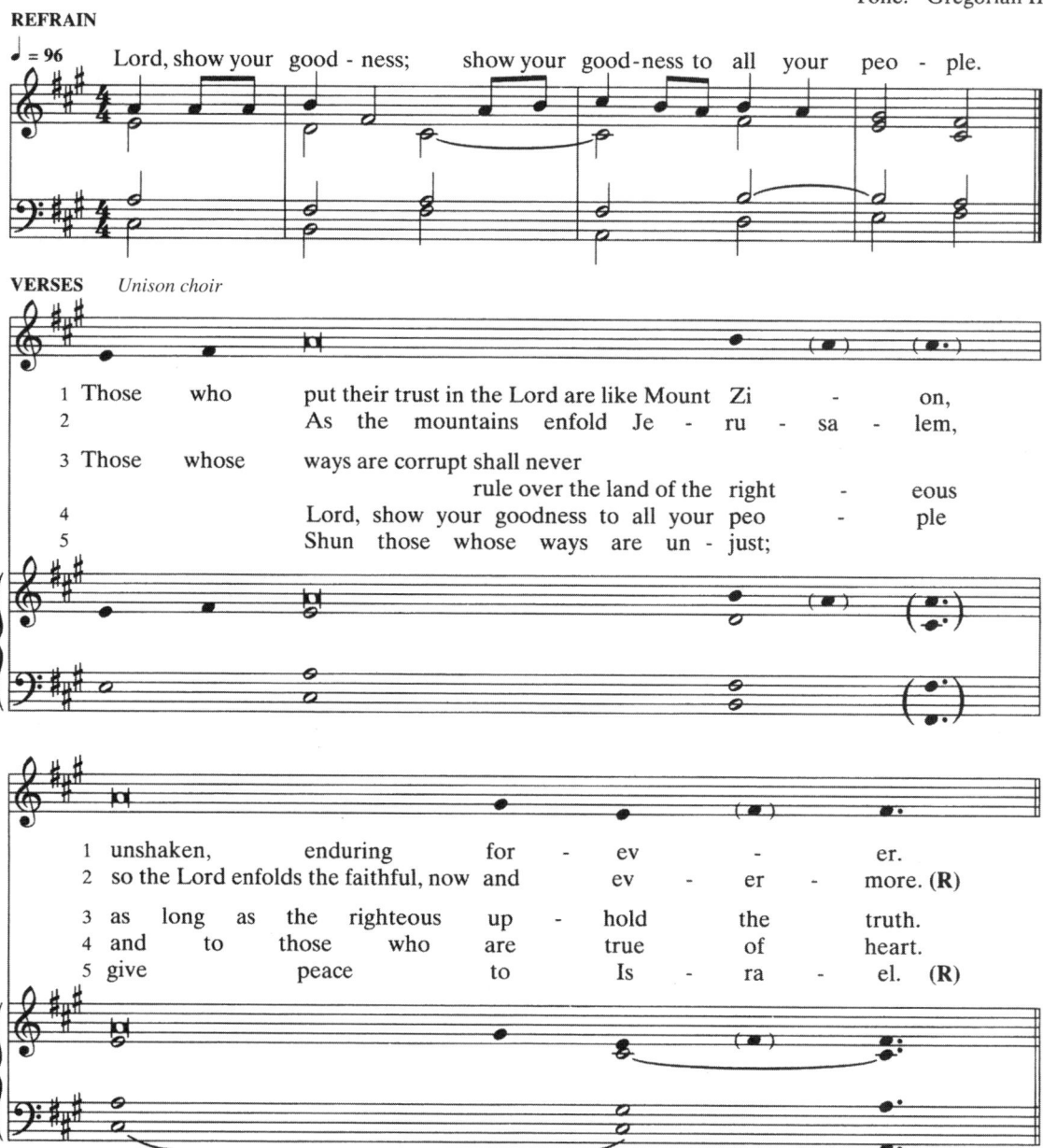

Copyright 1985 by Hope Publishing Company, Carol Stream, IL 60188. All rights reserved. Used by permission.

PSALM 126

The Grail — Joseph Gelineau

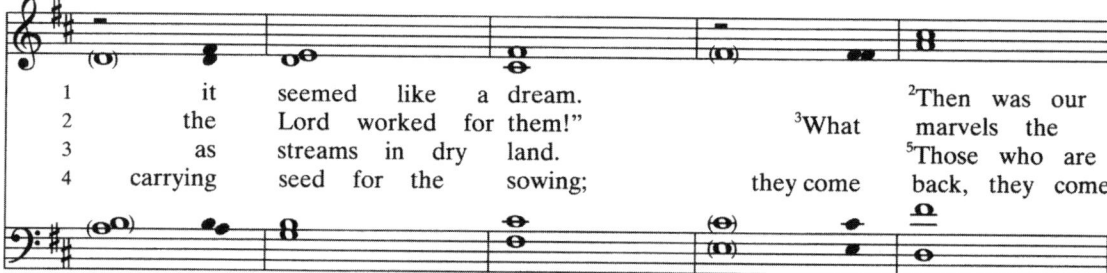

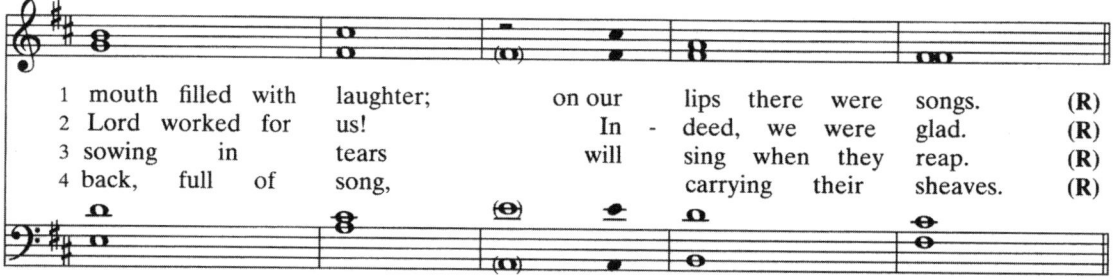

Text and music copyright 1963, 1986 The Grail, England, GIA Publications, Inc., exclusive North American agent, 7404 S. Mason Ave., Chicago, IL 60638. www.giamusic.com. 800.442.1358. All rights reserved. Used by permission.

PSALM 130

50

Hal H. Hopson Hal H. Hopson

REFRAIN

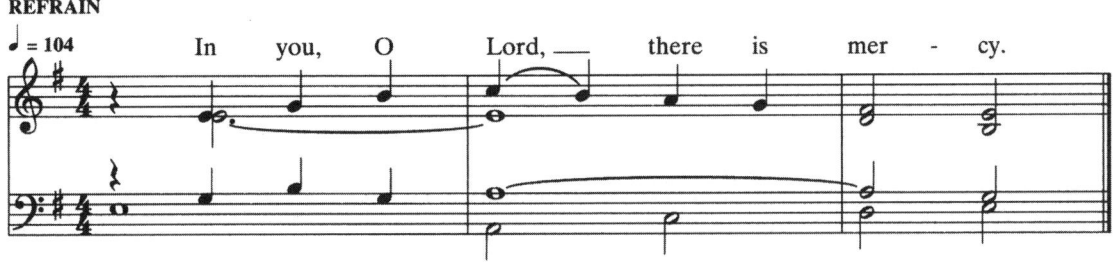

In you, O Lord, there is mercy.

VERSES

SATB choir (or cantor)

1 ¹Out of the depths I call to you, O Lord! ²Lord, hear my voice!
2 ³Should you, O Lord, remember all our sins, Lord, who could stand?
3 ⁵My soul waits for you, O Lord; in your word I hope.
4 ⁷May Israel wait for you, O Lord, for with you there is mercy.

1 Let your ears be at-tentive; Lord, hear my plea. (R)
2 ⁴But with you we are for-given; for this we worship you. (R)
3 ⁶My soul waits for you, O Lord, more than those who watch for the morning. (R)
4 With you there is full sal-vation; ⁸you will redeem Israel from all its sins. (R)

Copyright 1988 by Hope Publishing Company, Carol Stream, IL 60188. All rights reserved. Used by permission.

51   PSALM 131

Taizé   Jacques Berthier (Taizé)

REFRAIN
Put your hope in the Lord, both now and evermore.

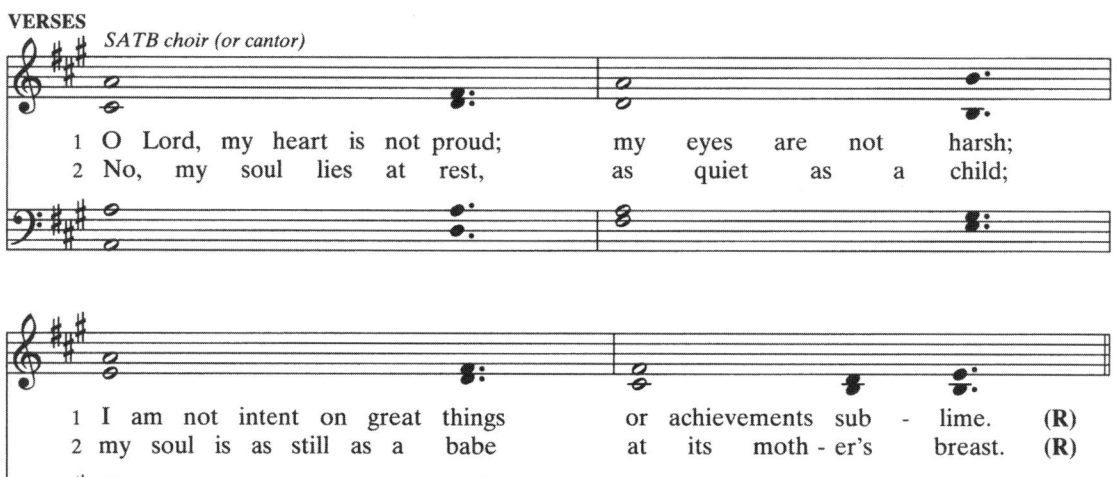

VERSES   *SATB choir (or cantor)*

1. O Lord, my heart is not proud; my eyes are not harsh;
   I am not intent on great things or achievements sublime. (R)
2. No, my soul lies at rest, as quiet as a child;
   my soul is as still as a babe at its mother's breast. (R)

Copyright 1982 Ateliers et Presses de Taizé, Taizé Community, France, GIA Publications, Inc., exclusive North American agent, 7404 S. Mason Ave., Chicago, IL 60638. www.giamusic.com. 800.442.1358. All rights reserved. Used by permission.

PSALM 133   52

Hal H. Hopson   Hal H. Hopson

Copyright 1989 by Hope Publishing Company, Carol Stream, IL 60188. All rights reserved. Used by permission.

Note: A more literal translation of the Chorus Refrain is: "For his great love is without end." This may be substituted if preferred.

Music © 1986 by GIA Publications, Inc.
Text © 1963, 1986 The Grail, England, GIA Publications, Inc., exclusive North American agent, 7404 S. Mason Ave., Chicago, IL 60638. www.giamusic.com. 800.442.1358. All rights reserved. Used by permission.

*Optional small orchestral wind chimes
**Optional gong

Copyright 1988 by Hope Publishing Company, Carol Stream IL 60188. All rights reserved. Used by permission.

55 PSALM 141

Arlo Duba John Weaver

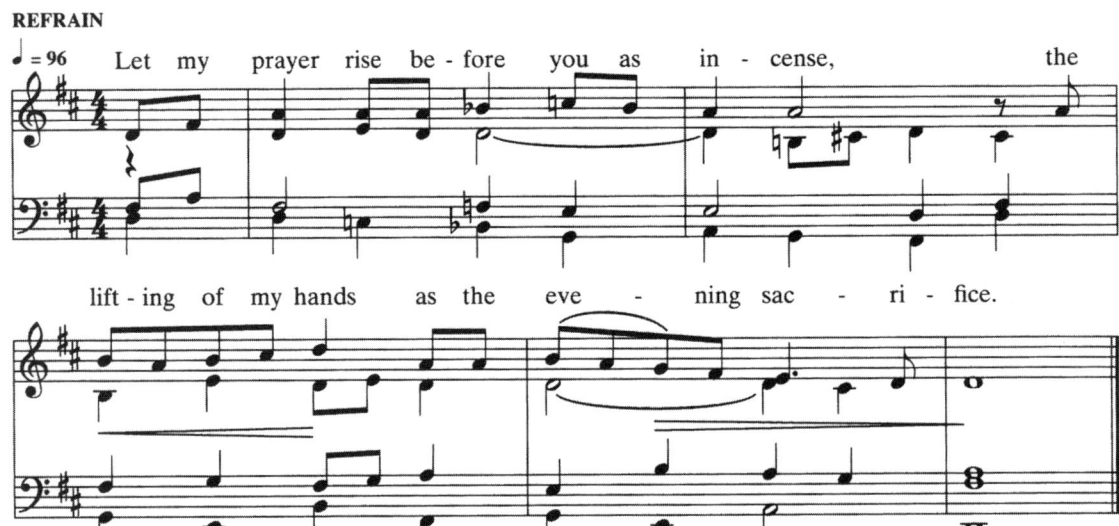

Text copyright 1986 Arlo D. Duba.
Music copyright 1987 John Weaver.
All rights reserved. Used by permission.

Copyright 1989 by Hope Publishing Comapny, Carol Stream, IL 60188. All rights reserved. Used by permission.

57

PSALM 145
(8–9, 18–19)

Hal H. Hopson *SATB choir*
Old Scottish Chant

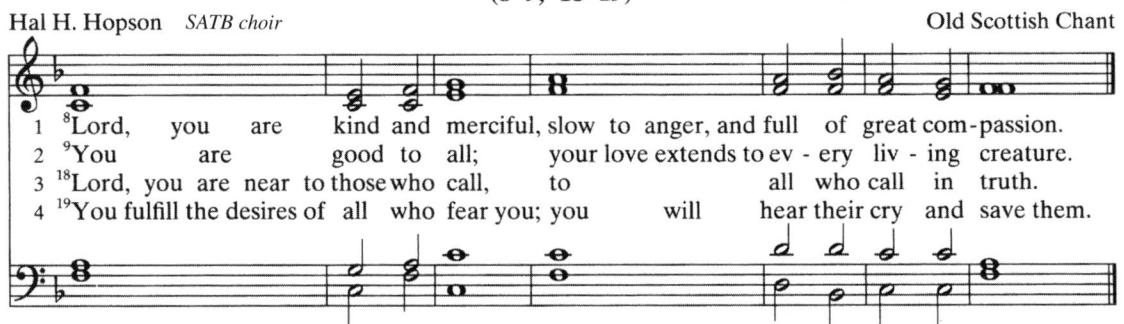

1 ⁸Lord, you are kind and merciful, slow to anger, and full of great compassion.
2 ⁹You are good to all; your love extends to every living creature.
3 ¹⁸Lord, you are near to those who call, to all who call in truth.
4 ¹⁹You fulfill the desires of all who fear you; you will hear their cry and save them.

Text copyright 1989 by Hope Publishing Company, Carol Stream, IL 60188. All rights reserved. Used by permission.

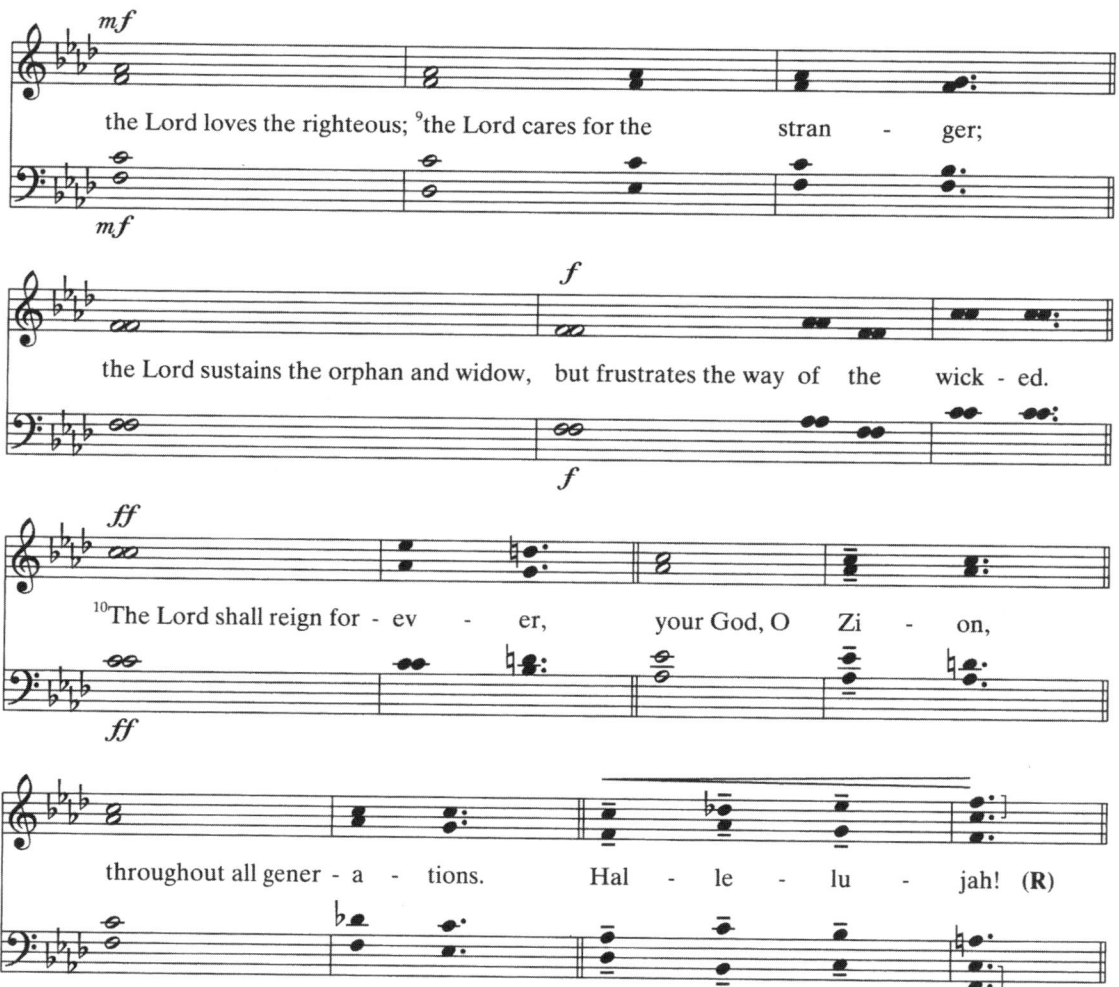

PSALM 147
(12–15, 19–20)

59

Hal H. Hopson

Hal H. Hopson

REFRAIN

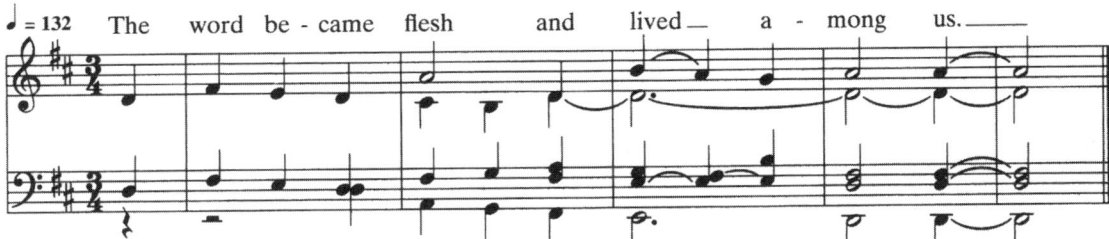

The word became flesh and lived among us.

VERSES

SATB choir (or cantor)

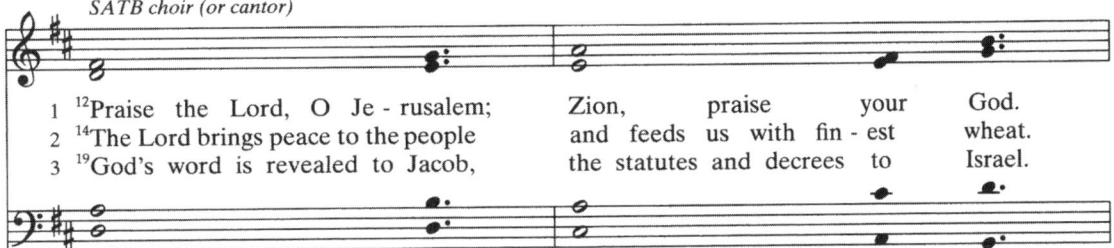

1 ¹²Praise the Lord, O Jerusalem;   Zion, praise your God.
2 ¹⁴The Lord brings peace to the people   and feeds us with finest wheat.
3 ¹⁹God's word is revealed to Jacob,   the statutes and decrees to Israel.

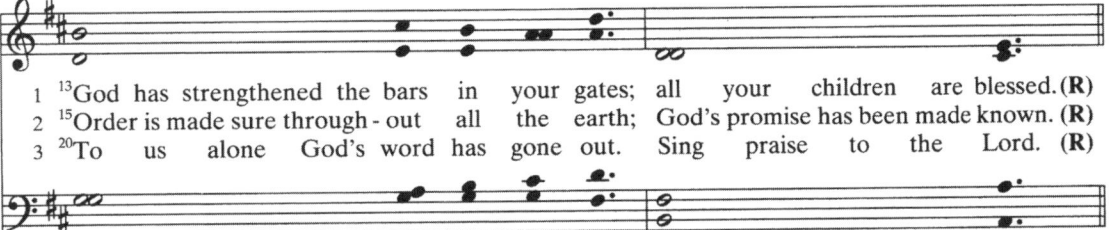

1 ¹³God has strengthened the bars in your gates; all your children are blessed. **(R)**
2 ¹⁵Order is made sure throughout all the earth; God's promise has been made known. **(R)**
3 ²⁰To us alone God's word has gone out. Sing praise to the Lord. **(R)**

Copyright 1989 by Hope Publishing Company, Carol Stream, IL 60188. All rights reserved. Used by permission.

PSALM 148

Commissioned for Northwoods Presbyterian Church Doraville, Georgia

Hal H. Hopson

REFRAIN

[Introduction ———————] Al-le - lu - ia! Al-le - lu - ia! Al-le - lu - ia!

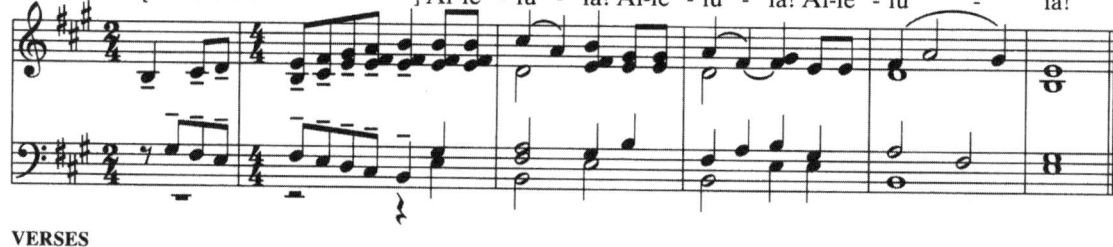

VERSES

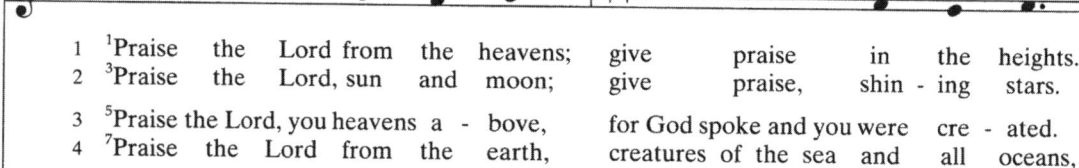

1 ¹Praise the Lord from the heavens; give praise in the heights.
2 ³Praise the Lord, sun and moon; give praise, shin - ing stars.
3 ⁵Praise the Lord, you heavens a - bove, for God spoke and you were cre - ated.
4 ⁷Praise the Lord from the earth, creatures of the sea and all oceans,
5 ⁹all moun - tains and hills, all fruit trees and cedars,
6 ¹¹all rul - ers and peoples, you that gov - ern the nations,
7 ¹³Praise the name of the Lord, for God alone is ex - alted.
8 ¹⁴God gives strength to the people. God be praised by all the saints,

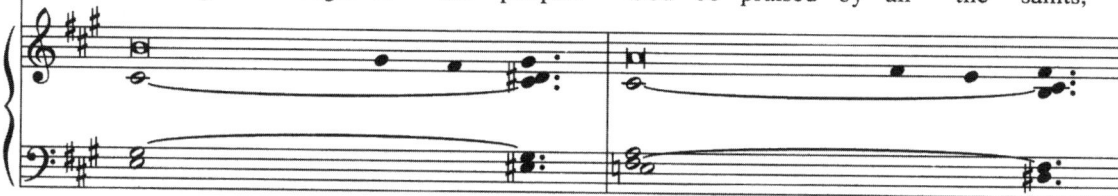

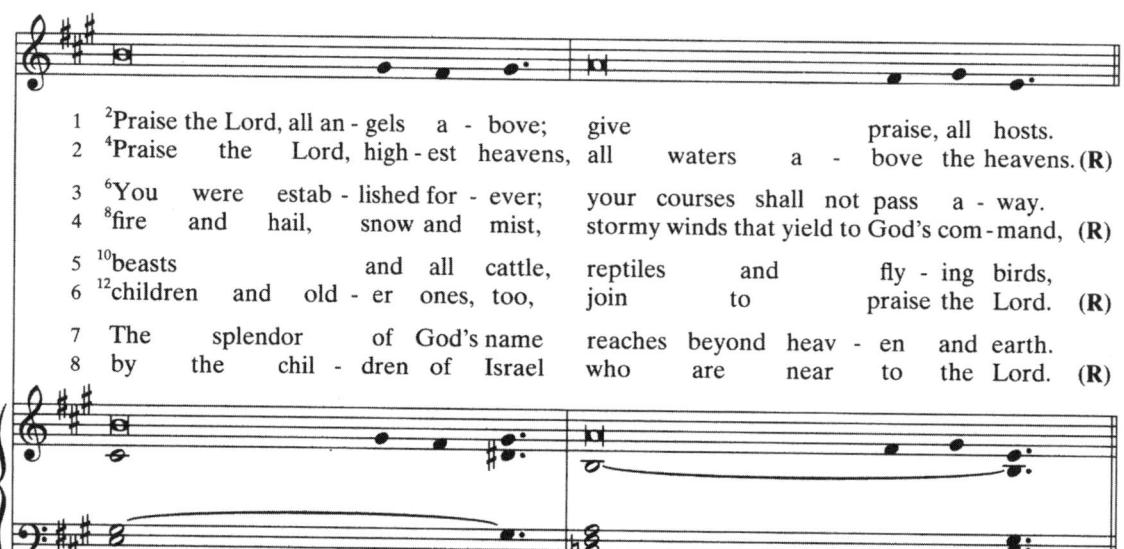

1 ²Praise the Lord, all an - gels a - bove; give praise, all hosts.
2 ⁴Praise the Lord, high - est heavens, all waters a - bove the heavens. (R)
3 ⁶You were estab - lished for - ever; your courses shall not pass a - way.
4 ⁸fire and hail, snow and mist, stormy winds that yield to God's com - mand, (R)
5 ¹⁰beasts and all cattle, reptiles and fly - ing birds,
6 ¹²children and old - er ones, too, join to praise the Lord. (R)
7 The splendor of God's name reaches beyond heav - en and earth.
8 by the chil - dren of Israel who are near to the Lord. (R)

Copyright 1988 by Hope Publishing Company, Carol Stream, IL 60188. All rights reserved. Used by permission.

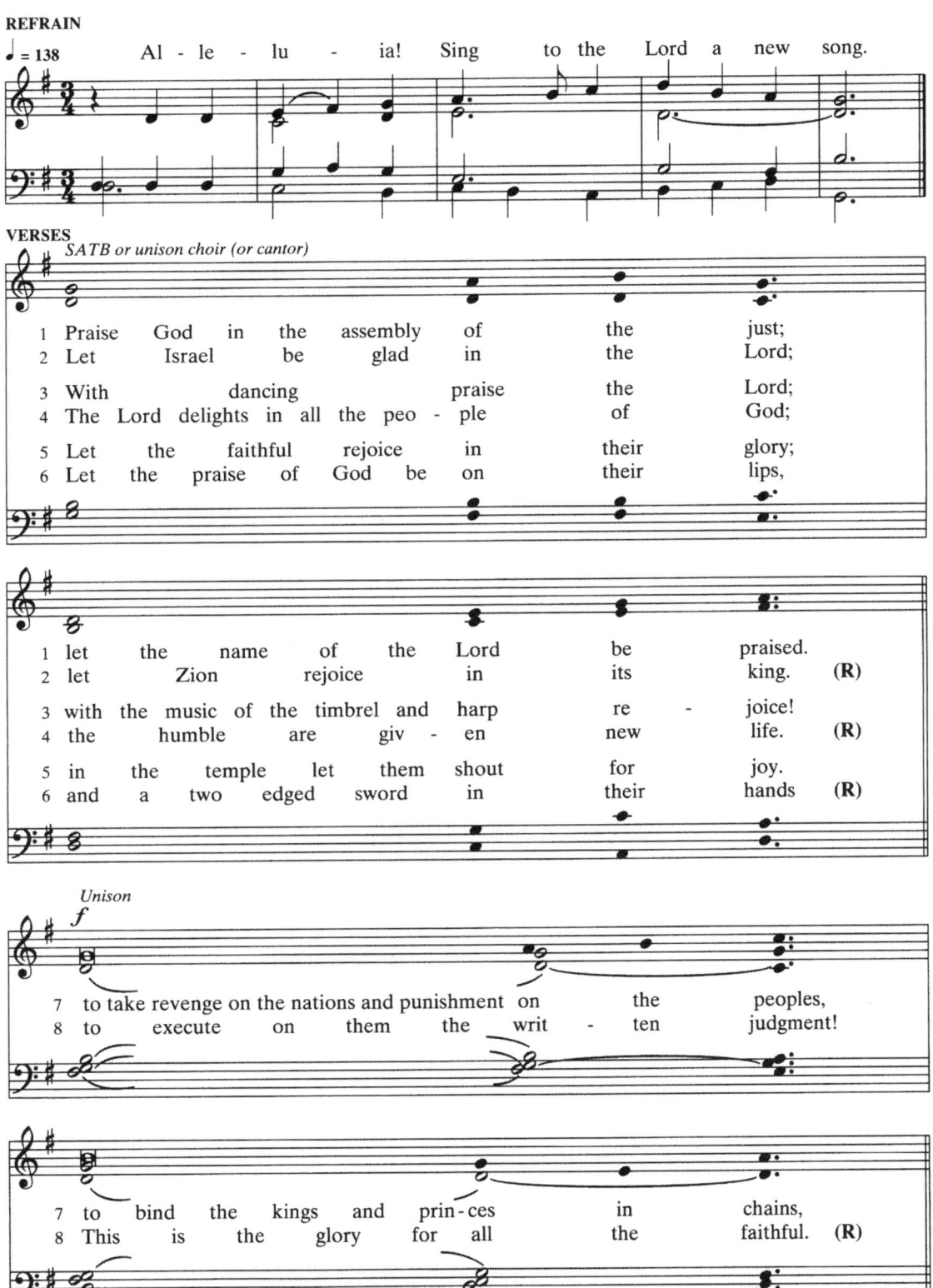

62

*Commissioned for
Northwoods Presbyterian Church
Doraville, Georgia*

PSALM 150

Hal H. Hopson Hal H. Hopson

Copyright 1990 by Hope Publishing Company, Carol Stream, IL 60188. All rights reserved. Used by permission.

CANTICLES AND ANCIENT HYMNS

63 CANTICLE OF ZECHARIAH (BENEDICTUS)
(Luke 1: 68–79)

English Language Liturgical Consultation

Byzantine Chant
arr. John Allyn Melloh, SM

REFRAIN

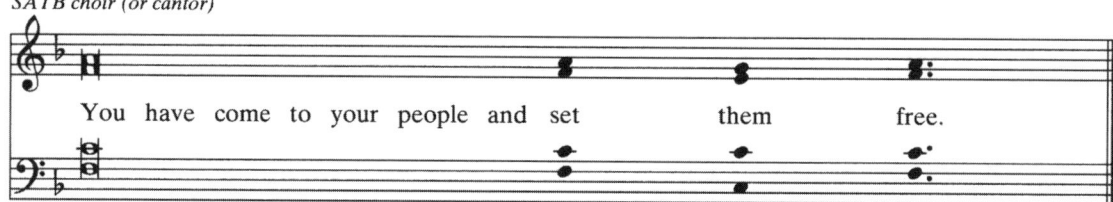

You have come to your people and set them free.

VERSES *SATB choir*

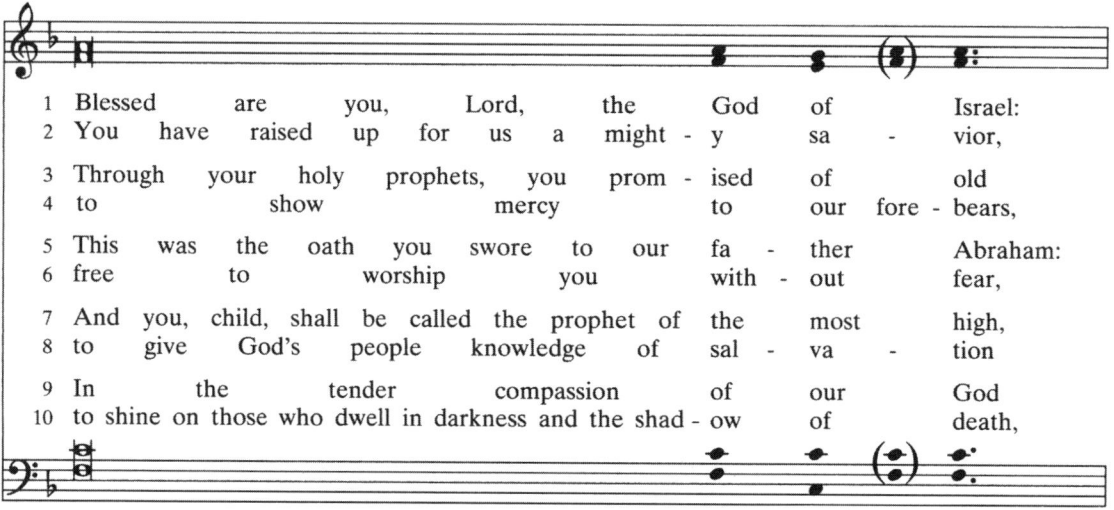

1. Blessed are you, Lord, the God of Israel:
2. You have raised up for us a might-y sa-vior,
3. Through your holy prophets, you prom-ised of old
4. to show mercy to our fore-bears,
5. This was the oath you swore to our fa-ther Abraham:
6. free to worship you with-out fear,
7. And you, child, shall be called the prophet of the most high,
8. to give God's people knowledge of sal-va-tion
9. In the tender compassion of our God
10. to shine on those who dwell in darkness and the shad-ow of death,

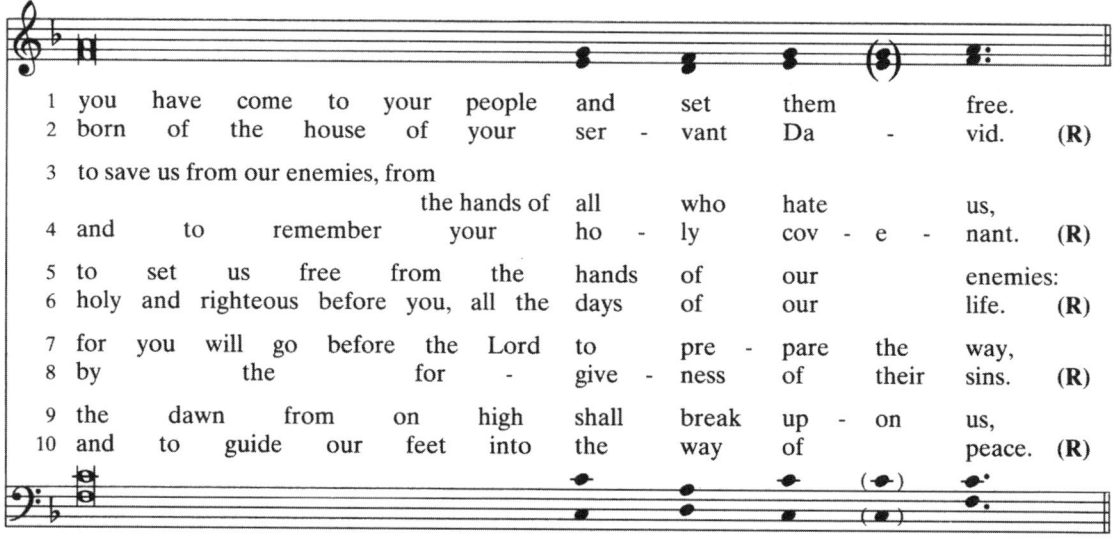

1. you have come to your people and set them free. **(R)**
2. born of the house of your ser-vant Da-vid. **(R)**
3. to save us from our enemies, from the hands of all who hate us,
4. and to remember your ho-ly cov-e-nant. **(R)**
5. to set us free from the hands of our enemies:
6. holy and righteous before you, all the days of our life. **(R)**
7. for you will go before the Lord to pre-pare the way,
8. by the for-give-ness of their sins. **(R)**
9. the dawn from on high shall break up-on us,
10. and to guide our feet into the way of peace. **(R)**

Music copyright 1979 by GIA Publications, Inc., 7404 S. Mason Ave.,
Chicago, IL 60638. www.giamusic.com. 800.442.1358. All rights reserved.
Used by permission.

CANTICLE OF ZECHARIAH (BENEDICTUS)
(Luke 1: 68–79)

English Language Liturgical Consultation
Howard Hughes, S.M.

REFRAIN
The rising sun will visit us with healing in its wings.

VERSES *SATB choir (or cantor)*

1. Blessed are you, Lord, the God of Israel; you have come to your people and set them free.
2. This was the oath you swore to your father Abraham: to set us free from the hands of our enemies,
3. In the tender compassion of our God the dawn from on high shall break upon us,

1. You have raised up for us a mighty savior, born of the house of your servant David.
2. free to worship you without fear, holy and righteous before you all the days of our life.

1. Through the holy prophets you promised of old to save us from our enemies, from the hands of all who hate us,
2. And you, child, shall be called the prophet of the most high, for you will go before the Lord to prepare the way,

1. to show mercy to our forebears, and to remember your holy covenant. (R)
2. to give God's people knowledge of salvation, for the forgiveness of their sins. (R)
3. to shine on those who dwell in darkness and the shadow of death, and to guide their feet into the way of peace. (R)

Music copyright 1979 by GIA Publications, Inc., 7404 S. Mason Ave., Chicago, IL 60638.
www.giamusic.com. 800.442.1358. All rights reserved. Used by permission.

65 CANTICLE OF SIMEON (NUNC DIMITTIS)
(Luke 2: 29–32)

English Language Liturgical Consultation, alt.
Hal H. Hopson

Solo, ensemble, or two-part choir

Now, Lord, you have kept your word: let your servant go in peace. With my own eyes I have seen the salvation which you have prepared in the sight of every people: a light to reveal you to the nations and the glory of your people Israel, Amen.

Choir, SATB with optional congregation in unison or SATB

Go now in peace. Go now in peace. Go now in peace. Go now in peace. Go now in peace. Go now in peace. Go now in peace. Go now in peace. Go now in peace. Amen.

Verses music and refrain copyright 1992 by Hope Publishing Company, Carol Stream, IL 60188. All rights reserved. Used by permission.

HYMN TO CHRIST AS LIGHT (PHOS HILARON) 66

Greek, c. 200
Tr. William G. Storey

David Clark Isele

1. O ra-diant Light, O Sun divine, of God the Father's deathless face, O Image of the Light sublime that fills the heavenly dwelling place.
2. O Son of God, the Source of life, praise is your due by night and day. Our happy lips must raise the strain of your esteemed and splendid name.
3. Lord Jesus Christ, as daylight fades, as shine the lights of eventide, we praise the Father with the Son, the Spirit blest, and with them one.

Text copyright 1979 by William G. Storey. All rights reserved. Used by permission. Accompaniment copyright 1986 by GIA Publications, Inc., 7404 S. Mason Ave., Chicago, IL 60638. www.giamusic.com. 800.442.1358. All rights reserved. Used by permission.

67 HYMN TO CHRIST AS LIGHT (PHOS HILARON)

Greek, c. 200
Tr. William G. Storey

JESU DULCIS MEMORIA
based on Gregorian II
Accomp. Richard Proulx

1. O radiant Light, O Sun divine, of God the Father's deathless face, O image of the Light sublime that fills the heavenly dwelling place.

2. O Son of God, the source of life, praise is your due by night and day. Our happy lips must raise the strain of your esteemed and splendid name.

3. Lord Jesus Christ, as daylight fades, as shine the lights of eventide, we praise the Father with the Son, the Spirit blest, and with them one.

Text copyright 1979 by William G. Storey. All rights reserved. Used by permission.
Accompaniment copyright 1975 by GIA Publications, Inc., 7404 S. Mason Ave., Chicago, IL 60638. www.giamusic.com. 800.442.1358. All rights reserved. Used by permission.

WE PRAISE YOU, O GOD (TE DEUM LAUDAMUS) 68

English Language Liturgical Consultation
Brother Reginald, S.S.F.

VERSES

1 We praise you, O God;
  we acclaim you as Lord;
  all creation worships you,
  the Father everlasting.

2 To you all angels, all the powers of heaven,
  the cherubim and seraphim, sing in endless praise:
  Holy, holy, holy Lord, God of power and might,
  heaven and earth are full of your glory.

3 The glorious company of apostles praise you.
  The noble fellowship of prophets praise you.
  The white-robed army of martyrs praise you.
  Throughout the world the holy church acclaims you:

4 Father, of majesty unbounded,
  your true and only Son, worthy of all praise,
  the Holy Spirit,
  advocate and guide.

5 You, Christ, are the king of glory,
  the eternal Son of the Father.
  When you took our flesh to set us free,
  you humbly chose the Virgin's womb.

6 You overcame the sting of death
  and opened the kingdom of heaven to all believers.
  You are seated at God's right hand in glory.
  We believe that you will come and be our judge.

7 Come then, Lord, and help your people,
  bought with the price of your own blood,
  and bring us with your saints
  to glory everlasting.

Music copyright The European Province of the Society of Saint Francis.

CANTICLE FROM LAMENTATIONS
(Lamentations 3: 19–26)

70

Vs. 19–21: *New Revised Standard Version*
Vs. 22–26: *A New Zealand Prayer Book*/He Karakia Mihinare o Aotearoa

John Weaver

Text (vss. 19–21) from the New Revised Standard Version of the Bible, copyright 1989 by the Division of Christian Education of the National Council of Churches of Christ in the USA. Used by permission.
Text (vss.22–26) copyright 1989 The Provincial Secretary, The Church in the Province of New Zealand.
Music copyright 1991 John Weaver. All rights reserved. Used by permssion.

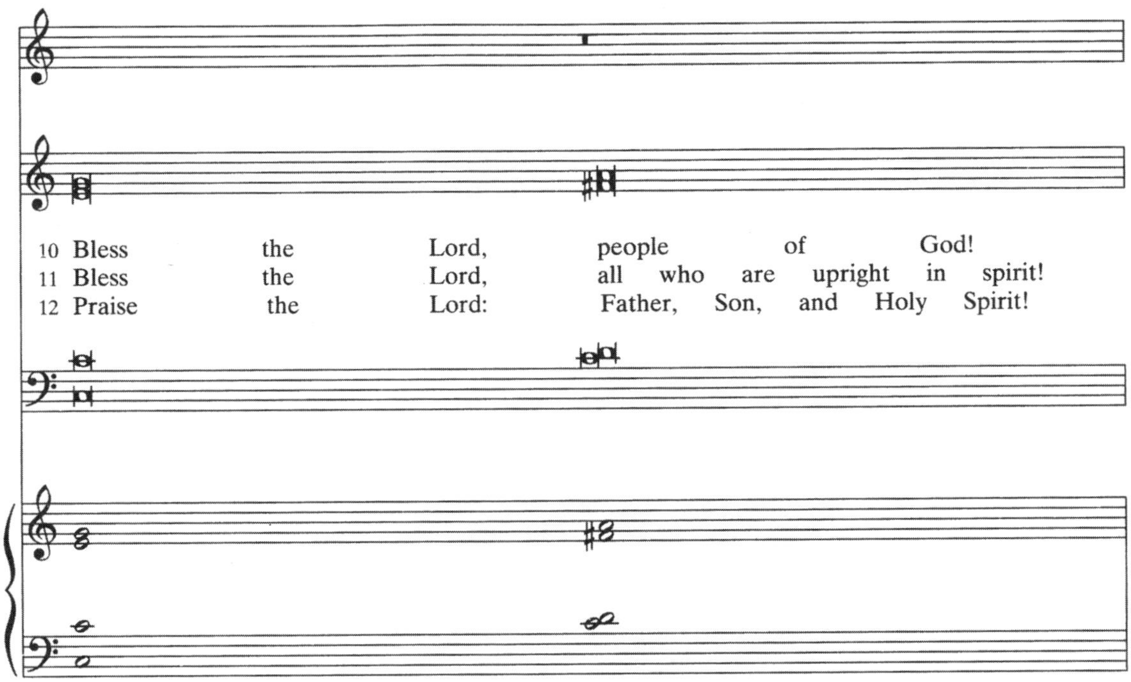

10 Bless the Lord, people of God!
11 Bless the Lord, all who are upright in spirit!
12 Praise the Lord: Father, Son, and Holy Spirit!

10 Priests and all who serve the Lord, bless the Lord! (R)
11 All who are holy and humble of heart, bless the Lord! (R)
12 Blessed are you, O Lord, in the vast expanse of heav - en! (R)

* **HANDBELLS NEEDED**

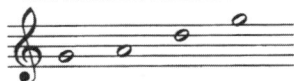

** *The verses should be chanted in speech rhythm, not in a rhythmic pulse.*

Verses music and refrain copyright 1987 by Hope Publishing Company, Carol Stream, IL 60188. All rights reserved. Used by permission.
Verses text copyright 1987 The Westminster Press.

CANTICLE OF CREATION
(Song of the Three Young Men 35–63)

The Grail
A. Gregory Murray

REFRAIN: To God be highest glory and praise for-ev-er.

VERSES (Cantor/Choir)

1. O all you works of the Lord, bless the Lord: (R)
2. And you, an-gels of the Lord, bless the Lord: (R)
3. And you, the hea-vens of the Lord, bless the Lord: (R)
4. And you, sun and moon, bless the Lord: (R)
5. And you, stars of the heavens, bless the Lord: (R)
6. And you, show-ers and rain, bless the Lord: (R)
7. And you, all breez-es and winds, bless the Lord: (R)
8. And you, cold and heat, bless the Lord: (R)
9. And you, night-time and day, bless the Lord: (R)
10. And you, moun-tains and hills, bless the Lord: (R)
11. And you, all plants of the earth, bless the Lord: (R)
12. And you, riv-ers and seas, bless the Lord: (R)
13. And you, crea-tures of the sea, bless the Lord: (R)
14. And you, ev-ery bird in the sky, bless the Lord: (R)
15. And you, wild beasts and tame, bless the Lord: (R)
16. And you, chil-dren of earth, bless the Lord: (R)
17. And you, priests of the Lord, bless the Lord: (R)
18. And you, ser-vants of the Lord, bless the Lord: (R)

Music © 1986 by GIA Publications, Inc.
Text © 1963, 1986 The Grail, England, GIA Publications, Inc., exclusive North American agent, 7404 S. Mason Ave., Chicago, IL 60638. www.giamusic.com. 800.442.1358. All rights reserved. Used by permission.

73 A CANTICLE OF PRAISE
(Song of the Three Young Men 29–34)

Book of Common Prayer
John Rutter

© Oxford University Press 1985. Reproduced by permission. All rights reserved.

74 A CANTICLE OF PENITENCE
(Prayer of Manasseh 1–2, 4, 6–7, 11-15)

Book of Common Prayer, alt.
Hal H. Hopson

REFRAIN
O Lord, you are full of com-pas-sion.

VERSES *SATB or unison choir (or cantor)*

1. O Lord and Ruler of the hosts of heaven, God of Abraham, Isaac, and Jacob,
2. O Lord, you are full of com-passion, [————————]
3. And now, O Lord, I bend the knee of my heart and make my ap-peal,
4. For you, O Lord, are the God of those who re-pent, [————————]

1. and all of their righteous offspring: you made the heaven and the earth
2. most patient, and abounding in mercy. You hold back your hand;
3. sure of your gracious goodness. I have sinned, O Lord; I have sinned,
4. and in me you show forth your goodness. Unworthy as I am you will save me

1. with all their vast ar-ray. All things quake with fear at your presence;
2. you do not punish as we de-serve. In your great good-ness, Lord,
3. and I know my wickedness all too well. Therefore I make my prayer to you:
4. in accordance with your great mercy, and I will praise you with-out ceasing

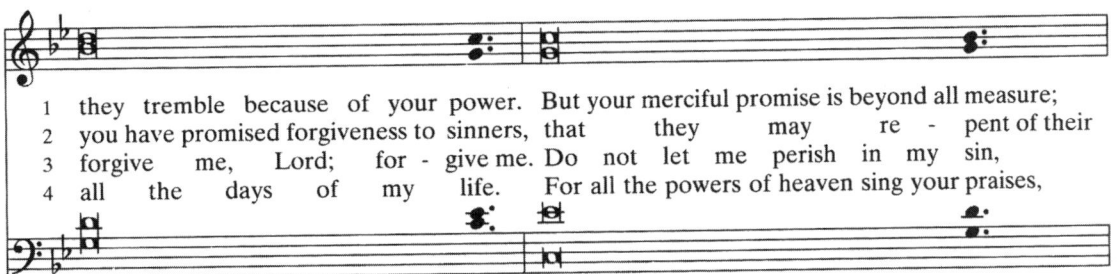

1 they tremble because of your power. But your merciful promise is beyond all measure;
2 you have promised forgiveness to sinners, that they may re - pent of their
3 forgive me, Lord; for - give me. Do not let me perish in my sin,
4 all the days of my life. For all the powers of heaven sing your praises,

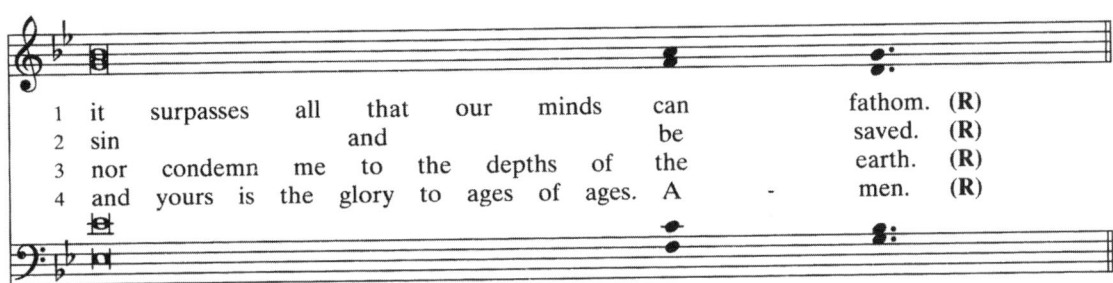

1 it surpasses all that our minds can fathom. (R)
2 sin and be saved. (R)
3 nor condemn me to the depths of the earth. (R)
4 and yours is the glory to ages of ages. A - men. (R)

Verses music and refrain copyright 1987 by Hope Publishing Company, Carol Stream, IL 60188. All rights reserved. Used by permission.

76 THE BEATITUDES
(Matthew 5: 3–12)

Jacques Berthier (Taizé)

*Latin pronunciation: Beh-ah-tee een daw-maw Daw-mee-nee

6 Blest are the pure in heart, for they shall see God. 7 Blest are the peace-mak-ers, for they shall be called the chil-dren of God. 8 Blest are those per-se-cu-ted for ho-li-ness sake, for theirs is the King-dom of heav-en.

* Choose either part

OPTIONAL SATB OSTINATO REFRAIN

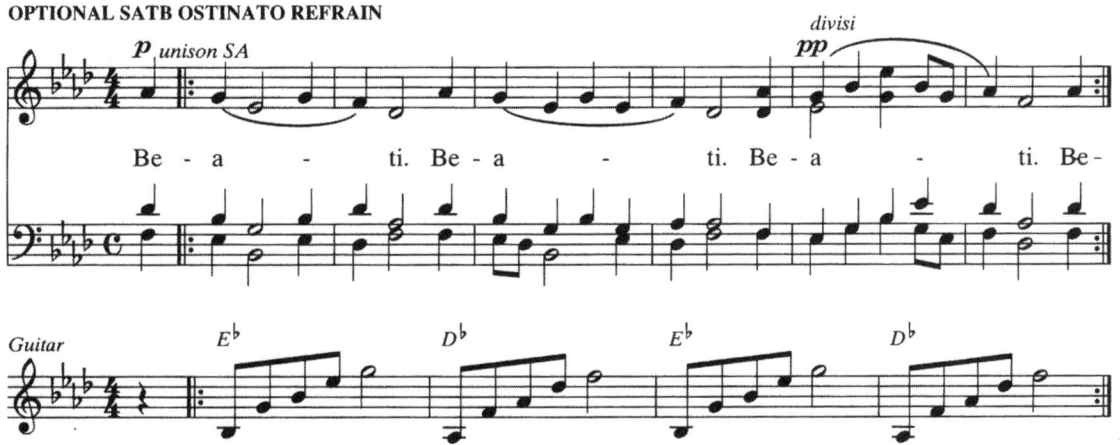

Be - a - ti. Be - a - ti. Be - a - ti. Be-

Text and music copyright 1982, Ateliers et Presses de Taizé, Taizé Community, France, GIA Publications, Inc., exclusive North American agent, 7404 S. Mason Ave., Chicago, IL 60638. www.giamusic.com. 800.442.1358. All rights reserved. Used by permission.

77 CHRIST OUR PASSOVER
(I Corinthians 5: 7–8;   Romans 6: 9–11;   I Corinthians 15: 20–22)

Book of Common Prayer, alt.

C. Hylton Stewart
Adapt. Hal H. Hopson

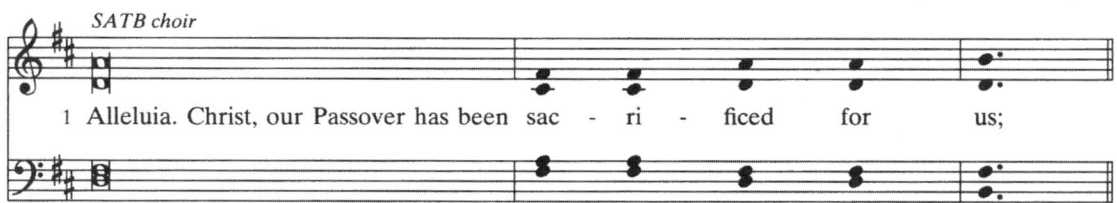
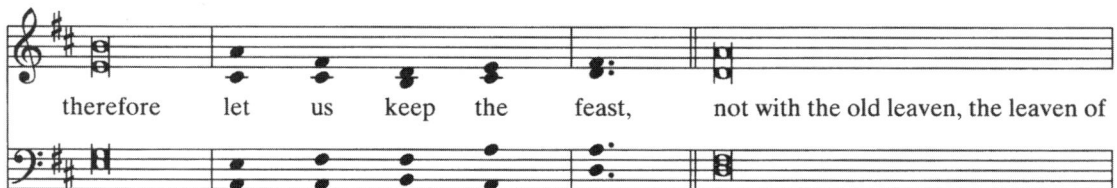
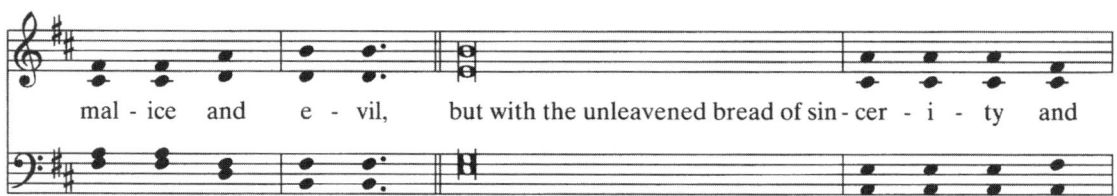
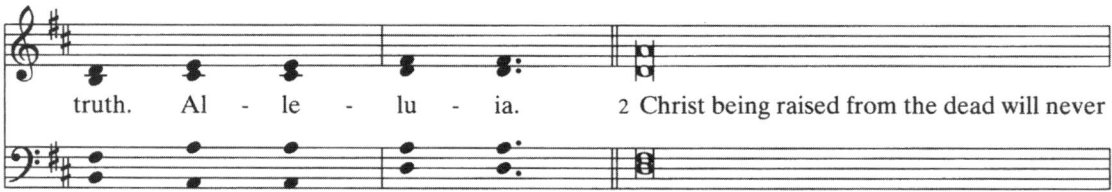
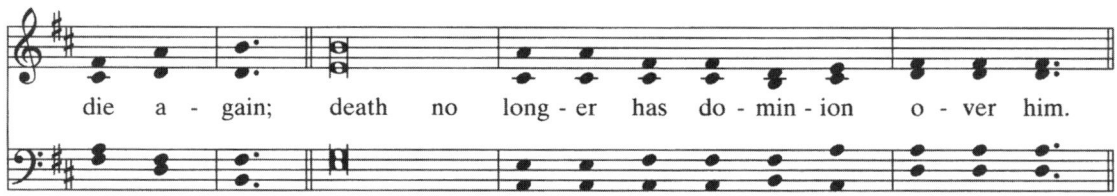

1 Alleluia. Christ, our Passover has been sacrificed for us; therefore let us keep the feast, not with the old leaven, the leaven of malice and evil, but with the unleavened bread of sincerity and truth. Alleluia.

2 Christ being raised from the dead will never die again; death no longer has dominion over him.

THE LORD'S PRAYER 79

English Language Liturgical Consultation

Plainsong Chant
Adapt. Hal H. Hopson
Accomp. Robert J. Batastini

Our Father in heaven, hallowed be your name, your kingdom come, your will be done, on earth as in heaven. Give us today our daily bread. Forgive us our sins as we forgive those who sin against us. Save us from the time of trial and deliver us from evil.

Accompaniment copyright 1986 by GIA Publications, Inc., 7404 S. Mason Ave., Chicago, IL 60638.
www.giamusic.com. 800.442.1358. All rights reserved. Used by permission.

THE LORD'S PRAYER

80

English Language Liturgical Consultation — Source unknown

1 Our Father in heaven, hallowed be your name,
2 Give us today our daily bread.
3 For the kingdom, the power,

1 your kingdom come,
2 Forgive us our sins as we forgive those who sin a - gainst us.
3 and the glory are yours,

1 your will be done, on earth as in heaven.
2 Save us from the time of trial and de-liver us from evil.
3 now and for - ever. A - men.

* *Optional harmony in smaller notes*